# Effective Program Practices

## for Underserved Gifted Students

*A CEC-TAG Educational Resource*

# Effective Program Practices

## for Underserved Gifted Students

### A CEC-TAG Educational Resource

*Cheryll M. Adams, Ph.D.,*
*and Cecelia A. Boswell, Ed.D.*

Series Editors
Cheryll M. Adams, Ph.D., Tracy L. Cross, Ph.D.,
Susan K. Johnsen, Ph.D., and Diane Montgomery, Ph.D.

PRUFROCK PRESS INC.
WACO, TEXAS

Library of Congress Cataloging-in-Publication Data

Adams, Cheryll, 1948-
 Effective program practices for underserved gifted students : a CEC-TAG educational resource / by Cheryll
M. Adams and Cecelia A. Boswell.
    p. cm.
 Includes bibliographical references.
 ISBN 978-1-59363-843-6 (pbk.)
 1. Gifted children--Education. 2. Gifted children--Identification. 3. Children with social disabilities--Edu-
cation. I. Boswell, Cecelia A., 1949- II. Title.
 LC3993.A33 2012
 371.95--dc23
                          2011029586

Edited by Jennifer Robins

Cover and layout design by Raquel Trevino

ISBN-13: 978-1-59363-843-6

Printed in the United States of America.

At the time of this book's publication, all facts and figures cited are the most current available. All telephone numbers, addresses, and websites URLs are accurate and active. All publications, organizations,
websites, and other resources exist as described in the book, and all have been verified. The authors and
Prufrock Press Inc. make no warranty or guarantee concerning the information and materials given out by
organizations or content found at websites, and we are not responsible for any changes that occur after
this book's publication. If you find an error, please contact Prufrock Press Inc.

Prufrock Press Inc.
P.O. Box 8813
Waco, TX 76714-8813
Phone: (800) 998-2208
Fax: (800) 240-0333
http://www.prufrock.com

# Table of Contents

Preface ...................................................................................vii

Chapter 1: Introduction to Effective Program Practices.............1

Chapter 2: Differentiation.......................................................11

Chapter 3: Acceleration..........................................................35

Chapter 4: Enrichment............................................................43

Chapter 5: Recommendations .................................................53

Suggested Resources...............................................................57

References ..............................................................................65

Appendix A: Overcoming Obstacles:
A Study of Inventors and Inventions (Grade 2)
*by Trisha Oswalt*........................................................................71

About the Authors.................................................................113

# Preface

This book is part of a special series from The Association for the Gifted (TAG), a division within the Council for Exceptional Children. Although the focus of this book is on effective program practices with underserved gifted populations, we acknowledge that we cannot discuss effective practices without considering the context of the students themselves and those who work with them. Thus, we examine these practices and how they impact students of poverty; students who are culturally, linguistically, and ethnically diverse; and students who are twice-exceptional.

We used a broad stroke to identify three practices that have empirical, theoretical, or practical evidence of effectiveness with gifted students: differentiation, enrichment, and acceleration. Because any one of these practices in and of itself—and, in some instances, components of the practice—can fill many pages, we have provided specific instances of effectiveness with the identified populations and have included a separate section of resources for further information about each one.

Because we both have experience as teachers and administrators, we felt it was vital to include practical ideas, sample lessons, and a unit in an effort to assist busy professionals with implementing some of our suggestions. We hope our readers will find opportunities to use these materials. We particularly thank teacher Trisha Oswalt, who allowed us to include her unit in this book.

# CHAPTER 1

# Introduction to Effective Program Practices

This book will provide coordinators, teachers, administrators, parents, and other interested parties information about effective program practices for underserved gifted students. The population of underserved gifted students includes those who are culturally, linguistically, and ethnically diverse (CLED); those who come from poverty; and those who are twice-exceptional (2e). Thus, we use the terms *underrepresented* and *underserved* to encompass all of these groups. These groups of students have historically been underrepresented in gifted programs for a variety of reasons, such as schools using poor identification practices, offering a lack of appropriate programming, and viewing these students through the lens of a deficit model. Other publications in this series provide a full discussion of these issues; our focus is to describe and provide examples of effective program practices that might be used to increase academic achievement of and provide opportunities for underserved students to demonstrate their talent potential.

Based on the underrepresentation of various oppressed groups such as non-White and non-Asian (e.g., Ford, Grantham, & Milner, 2004) and poor and working-class children (e.g., Borland & Wright, 1994) in gifted education programs today, it is evident that not much has changed since the early days of gifted education. According to Latz and Adams (2010),

> It is important to note here that while [we] acknowledge and accept that giftedness is a cultural construction as asserted by

Margolin (1994a, 1994b) and Borland (1997), [we] also concede that the concept of giftedness as an absolute category of individuals operates and exists within life in real ways. That schools have different definitions of giftedness as well as different mechanisms in place to sort students into categories of gifted and non-gifted illustrates that the concept is in fact a cultural construction and an operational reality. (p. 4)

Paying attention to differences among groups of students is a step toward leveling the academic playing field. When teachers target their lessons only on issues of the dominant culture and focus on students who do not have other exceptionalities, then they leave out what may be the majority of our students. The literature addressing students who are culturally, linguistically, and ethnically diverse and students who come from poverty delineates several issues that are critical for these students to be successful. Among these are access to high-quality curriculum and instruction (Boykin, 2000; Denbo, 2002; Ladson-Billings, 1995; Rance-Roney, 2004; Renzulli & Reis, 2006; VanTassel-Baska, 2010) and a nurturing learning environment (Delisle, 2008; Ford & Grantham, 2003; Tomlinson, 2008). These issues hold true for students who are gifted and have an additional exceptionality such as a learning disability. Just as the twice-exceptional child may struggle in classrooms and assessment situations due to a learning disability, other gifted children may struggle with poverty, English as a second language, and/or cultural differences. What often happens is that these factors may interfere with the identification of these children as gifted, thus denying them the services necessary for academic or intellectual growth commensurate with their abilities.

The school culture preserves and reifies certain structures that often work against our underserved populations by not giving legitimate attention to certain gender, race, and class interests. Thus, students who "embody the dominant culture are affirmed by the curriculum and exist comfortably within the . . . school setting. Conversely, students who do not embody the dominant culture may find themselves in an oppressive, constrained, and uncomfortable situation" (Latz & Adams, 2010, p. 13). The latter scenario can result in student apathy, resentment, and disengagement (McLaren, 2003). VanTassel-Baska (2010) identified several directions that appear promising when developing effective interventions for special population learners:

1. Separate instructional opportunities for students with the same developmental profile.
2. The use of technology, especially microcomputers, to aid in transmission of learning for many special population learners.
3. Small-group and individual counseling, mentorships, and internships for special population learners.
4. A focus on the arts as a therapeutic intervention as well as a creative and expressive outlet.
5. Use of materials rich in ideas and imagination coupled with emphasis on higher level skills. (p. 199)

It is evident that teachers need to look at these underserved students through a different lens and reconceptualize their notions of teaching and learning. For example, Gallavan (2000) found more than 50 reasons teachers do not use effective practices with these students, particularly CLED students. From these reasons, several trends were identified, including teachers' lack of understanding of effective practices, lack of motivation to learn these practices, and lack of responsibility for using these practices (Gallavan, 2000). We hope this book will provide the motivation, knowledge, understanding, and skills to encourage teachers to implement effective program practices in the classroom for underserved populations of gifted students, to assist parents in being advocates for their children, and to alert administrators and counselors to the potential barriers that can exist for these students. Callahan (2007) suggested the creation of a "Master Adult Triad" consisting of parent, teacher, and mentor as a way to support and nurture students who are gifted and from underserved populations. For our purposes, we would consider the counselor as a member of the triad to coexist with or take the place of a mentor. From mathematics we know that the strongest support comes from the triangle, thus this triad is a strong support for these students. Should one member of the triad not be able to function as effectively at any given time, the remaining members can keep the power of the triad intact. Using the triangle metaphor and the knowledge shared in this publication, educational stakeholders can provide challenging, meaningful, and appropriate educational experiences for all students.

# EFFECTIVE PRACTICES

In this book, we use a broad definition of *effective practices*. We discuss those that have been found to be effective through research, theory, or practice, including professional wisdom and emerging practice at the classroom level. We identify three broad areas of effective practices—differentiation, acceleration, and enrichment—and acknowledge these three are interrelated. Thus, we have not set out to create an artificial trichotomy or to oversimplify these practices. For the sake of looking at elements that are both similar and different among them, we will define and discuss these practices individually and collectively, keeping in mind that they are interrelated.

We note that these three broad areas of practices fit nicely into the Response to Intervention (RtI) model. The traditional RtI model designed for struggling learners is a triangle defined through three levels of intervention: Tiers 1, 2, and 3. According to The Association for the Gifted's (TAG, 2010) position paper on RtI and gifted children,

> The use of the RTI framework for gifted students would support advanced learning needs of children in terms of a faster paced, more complex, greater depth and/or breadth with respect to their curriculum and instruction. It should also be noted that students who are gifted with disabilities may need more than one level of intervention and advancement in terms of curriculum and instructional strategies. (pp. 1–2)

Some RtI models address gifted students through the three tiers, and others have adapted the triangle by making it inverted, adding an internal circle, or expanding it to a vertical or horizontal diamond. All models include efforts to meet the needs of students who struggle in different ways. Gifted and talented learners struggle against sameness, repetitive content and practice, and boredom borne from learning that is inappropriate in strategy and content. Twice-exceptional and CLED gifted learners also struggle against these. Response to Intervention offers an opportunity to address their learning needs as well as their learning strengths.

Generally, RtI's three levels are designed to accommodate learners in the general education classroom (Tier 1), with universal interventions to the core program that are both preventative and proactive. For gifted learners from underserved populations, this can be in the form of whole-class activities that are built on higher level thinking. For example, the students may explore a learning concept with the teacher using Socratic questioning to lead discussions, or the teacher may develop tiered activities and assignments to meet the needs of all levels of learning in the class.

Tier 2 provides targeted interventions for 5%–10% of the students, those who were unresponsive to interventions in Tier 1. Examples of effective practices at this level for our target population include differentiation and/or enrichment within cluster groups with the help of a professional to further accommodate learning needs. For example, the students could work in a cluster group of gifted students who are creating a project that meets their learning strengths while the professional makes modifications that allow the 2e or CLED learner to express ideas and products at the level of the other gifted students.

Tier 3, intensive interventions, is designed for the 1%–5% of students who have not responded to interventions at Tiers 1 and 2. Target students at this level may work on an independent study with the help of a professional who can address specific learning needs and at the same time respect learning strengths and interests, or these learners may be accelerated in a particular subject area of strength. According to the TAG (2010) position paper,

> A flexible system of continuous and comprehensive services allows schools to meet the needs of gifted students at varying levels of development. In this way, services are less dependent on a student's label and more dependent on a student's need. (pp. 3–4)

Because providing the same level of instruction with the same materials at the same time for all children in the classroom is not an effective practice, specific elements must be in place before teachers can effectively have students doing different work in the same classroom. Thus, before we begin our discussion of specific practices, we want to take a moment to talk about those elements.

According to Adams and Pierce (2006), four components promote success when modifying the instruction for different learners: classroom management, anchoring activities, differentiated assessment, and accommodations. If any component is lacking, chaos can overshadow even the most exciting lesson.

# CLASSROOM MANAGEMENT

Classroom management is an art, and anyone who has taught even a few days knows how vital it is for this component to be in place for teaching and learning to occur. Rules for safe classroom behavior as well as directions for performing daily routines are commonly found in most classrooms. However, in a classroom where different students are working on different activities, classroom management becomes even more critical. In addition to rules and routines, strategies that allow the teacher to direct multiple groups of children working on different activities are necessary. Students need to understand how to work independently (alone or in a group), how to access materials when needed, and how to let the teacher know they need assistance when the teacher is working with another group. In general, students don't arrive in classrooms knowing how to work in a group, thus the teacher must spend time teaching the children how to work in a classroom where differentiation is occurring. They may use a variety of techniques such as "ask three before me" and "6-inch voices"; attention-getting devices such as a red cup on the desk for "help needed" and a green cup for "I'm fine on my own"; individual timers; and other management ideas that allow them to work with one group or an individual while the rest of the students work on their own. (For further discussion of classroom management in a differentiated classroom, see Adams and Pierce, 2006, and Tomlinson, 2001.)

# ANCHORING ACTIVITIES

The use of anchoring activities, which are activities that students do when they have completed their assigned work or are waiting for teacher assistance, is another critical piece to successful management in a classroom where students are working on different assignments at different paces. A variety of options come under the category of anchoring activities. These may be, but are not limited to, activities for review or enrichment, time to work on a self-selected project, opportunities to work at learning centers, self-selected reading, and content-based problem-solving activities. (For a full discussion of anchoring activities in a differentiated classroom, see Adams and Pierce, 2006, and Tomlinson, 2001.)

# DIFFERENTIATED ASSESSMENT

When students differ in their readiness, interest, or learning profile, then providing the same assessment for everyone doesn't make much sense. Common sense tells teachers that this variation is true, but with the emphasis in many classrooms on grade-level standards and curriculum, as well as electronic submission of grades so that parents may view them daily, teachers have to be creative in reconciling their effective use of differentiated assessments within the constraints of such standardization. Teachers may develop assessments that have some common items that all students must know, understand, and be able to do while adding other components to meet the needs of those students who were accelerated or received enrichment. Having multiple forms of a particular assessment, then, would not be uncommon.

Both formative and summative assessments are necessary data-gathering instruments to determine where students are and where they need to move next. Some assessments are embedded directly in daily instruction. Homework assignments and exit cards are good examples of embedded assessment used to gather student data; responses to these measures assist the teacher in determining who is ready for the next lesson and who is lost.

Pre- and postassessments play vital roles as two sides of the same coin. Before beginning a unit of instruction, the teacher uses a preassessment to determine who has already mastered the material, who knows some of the material, and who has little to no previous knowledge of the topic. Using the preassessment scores, teachers can then provide enrichment or acceleration for those who already know the material and plan other learning options for those who don't. Postassessments are planned so that students may demonstrate the knowledge, skills, and understandings they have learned about the material studied. Clearly, if students study different materials, they will need to have different assessments. Sometimes teachers think of a postassessment as simply a paper-and-pencil unit test; however, projects designed to target the same learning goals and objectives as a test allow students to show what they have learned using a different format. A clearly articulated, well-designed rubric that delineates the criteria for the project can gather the same data as a paper-and-pencil test. (For more information about differentiated assessment, see Adams and Pierce, 2006, and Tomlinson, 2001.)

# ACCOMMODATIONS

Other considerations that must be evident for educational practices to be effective include appropriate accommodations for students who require them. For some students to be successful, it may mean the use of technology or adaptive devices. For others, the use of an instructional aide, a translator, or a resource teacher is necessary for them to have access to instructional materials at levels commensurate with their intellectual and academic ability. Scaffolding may need to be provided for those who are missing foundational concepts due to lack of exposure rather than lack of ability. Only when educators, parents, counselors, and administrators recognize that allowing these accommodations does not equate with some students receiving special attention can educational practices be effective with all students. Just as teachers would not deny a child the use of eyeglasses or a hearing aid, teachers must not prohibit other accommodations that allow the child to thrive in the classroom despite exceptionalities, cultural diversity, or poverty.

# SUMMARY

No matter which practice teachers may choose to use for a specific learner or group of learners, teachers must keep in mind that no one practice works for everyone. Some learners may need multiple accommodations, and others may just need a few simple modifications to the general curriculum for challenging, meaningful learning to occur. The following steps are suggested for making decisions about effective practices for twice-exceptional learners (Montgomery County Public Schools, 2004):

- Analyze what the roles and responsibilities of the educators are within the school.
- Assign the roles and responsibilities to the educators within the school.
- Set a collaborative climate. Team planning facilitates inclusion of the students who are GT/LD in the general education classroom.
- Collect and study data related to the students (IEPs; tests; GT screening data scores; teachers, staff, and parent observations; students' inventories).
- Focus on students' strengths and interests.
- Analyze curriculum to identify key concepts.
- Collect resources and materials (curriculum guides, programs, and software).
- Choose appropriate resources, materials, strategies, and techniques.
- Plan for alternative learning activities.
- Plan units and lessons.
- Identify appropriate adaptations and accommodations for each student.
- Implement units and lessons.
- Plan for assessments that capitalize on students' strengths and obviate weaknesses.
- Evaluate successful/best practices.
- Schedule team meetings to discuss students. Specific weekly, bimonthly or monthly meeting times allow for ongoing planning

and an opportunity to discuss and evaluate student progress. Difficulties are addressed before they multiply and escalate.

- In-service/train teachers on GT/LD characteristics, needs, strategies, adaptations, and accommodations.
- In-service/train students and parents on resources, materials, and strategies when needed.
- Keep lines of communication open among staff, students, and parents. (p. M-1)

Likewise, Tomlinson and Strickland (2004) identified seven themes from the literature that serve to ensure that CLED students have access to challenging and meaningful educational opportunities:

- understand how culture affects teaching and learning;
- understand and address the role of student expectations in the education of students of color;
- demonstrate an immutable belief, translated into consistent action, that students of color will succeed academically at high levels;
- understand and ensure the centrality of high quality curriculum in the success of students of color;
- develop policies and programs that support success for students of color in multiple ways;
- develop environments that are supportive and nurturing of students of color; and
- persist for meaningful change. (p. 36)

Teachers must keep in mind these issues as they select, modify, and use effective practices to challenge gifted learners from underserved populations. (For an excellent summary of the research on instructional planning and instructional strategies, see Johnsen, 2008, pp. 25–26 and 28–29.)

# CHAPTER 2

# Differentiation

Differentiated instruction is an approach to teaching and learning that is proactive and flexible, and it provides multiple pathways for student learning (Tomlinson, 2001). This philosophy takes into account that students bring to the classroom a variety of learner characteristics that teachers must honor if they are to provide the most appropriate learning environment for all students. Differentiation involves modifying the content, process, product, learning environment, and affect to meet the needs of all learners, including gifted learners. More often than not, students with gifts and talents are in the general education classroom. Even when students who have gifts and talents are placed in homogeneous configurations such as cluster groups, special classes, or special schools, differentiation is still the key to meeting their needs. Students with gifts and talents do not constitute a single, easily identified population; they are academically diverse with their own individual set of learning characteristics and needs. Differentiation emphasizes having developmentally appropriate lessons that provide students with choice and a moderate challenge. Students should not be required to continually repeat something they have already learned. Their learning activities should be engaging, meaningful, and worthy of their time, and a variety of instructional strategies should be employed to assist with learning.

*Differentiation* is the term educators of the gifted use in the same way special education professionals use *modification*. Both terms reflect adjusted required curriculum to allow for differences in learning preferences, strengths, and needs. For many underserved gifted students, only modification is addressed. For gifted students who are CLED, those who come from poverty, and those who are twice-exceptional, both terms are applicable. To assure that these students are given appropriate curriculum opportunities, it is vital that teachers take into consideration the effects of social class, poverty, ethnicity, and learning exceptionalities when they modify the curriculum for gifted learners.

# LEARNING CHARACTERISTICS

Unique learning characteristics of gifted students are the basis for differentiation (Maker 1982; Renzulli & Reis, 2004, 2006; Tomlinson, 2003; VanTassel-Baska, 2010). Issues of language, culture, ethnicity, interests, exceptionality, family background, and learning profile all impact individual learners in different ways (Johnsen, 2008). When planning educational opportunities for those from underserved populations, teachers must be cognizant that the profiles of these learners will be uneven. Accommodating their strengths while being sensitive to their areas that are not yet as strongly developed requires advanced planning. In addition, input from parents, counselors, and community members can assist teachers in understanding the issues that surround underserved populations (VanTassel-Baska, 2010). When developing academic interventions for underserved populations, whether these involve enrichment or acceleration, teachers need to keep in mind the following learner characteristics possessed by these students as synthesized by VanTassel-Baska (2010):

- openness to experience;
- nonconforming, independence in thinking;
- creativity and fluency in their thinking;
- preference for oral expression;
- quickness to blend feelings with thoughts;
- responsiveness to multiple modes of learning as displayed in the arts;
- preference for hands-on applications;
- preference for real-world connections; and
- responsiveness to individual learning patterns. (p. 198)

Knowing the learning characteristics of students who are twice-exceptional is also vital if educational practices are to be effective. Students who are twice-exceptional may have weaknesses in processing, motor skills, memory, or reading or math skills for their grade level. According to the Montgomery County Public Schools' (2004) guidebook for twice-exceptional students, these issues

> are likely to impact their access to rigorous instruction across all subject areas. In planning, it is crucial that the teacher consider instructional methods and strategies that either circumvent students' difficulties or that build in the necessary scaffolding to empower students to be successful with the demands of the assignment. (p. M-1)

(For an excellent summary of research on individual learning differences, see Johnsen, 2008, pp. 24–25 for a discussion of Standard 3 of the National Gifted Education Standards.)

# CONTENT, PROCESS, PRODUCT, AFFECT, AND LEARNING ENVIRONMENT

Differentiation encompasses what is taught (*content*), how students learn new information (*process*), the ways students express and evaluate their learning (*product*), methods and experiences that elicit the best effort from students (*learning environment*), and learning experiences and preferences students bring with them to the classroom (*affect*). Differentiation matches learning preferences and strengths of the student within curriculum content, process, product, affect, and environment (Berger, 1991; Gallagher et al., 1976; Tomlinson, 2001, 2003). Differentiation for twice-exceptional and other underrepresented learners addresses these five areas.

## CONTENT

Differentiation of content (ideas, descriptive information, and facts) has been described as the process of modification through conceptual learning, interdisciplinary content presentation, acceleration, pacing, and curriculum compacting (Berger, 1991; Kaplan, 2008; Tomlinson, 2001, 2003).

**Conceptual learning.** Differentiation of content includes concept-based learning with a broad-based theme (concept) and an essential understanding that focuses on the concept and creates the purpose for learning. The brain understands and organizes efficiently when it comprehends through categories, understands the how and why of ideas, and makes comparisons (Caine & Caine, 1991; Erickson, 2002, 2007); it is pattern-seeking and concepts are pattern makers. Concepts help the brain create systems of organization that promote thinking and information storage and retrieval. Concept-based learning addresses the needs of gifted learners, who process information through this broad view—the big picture or concept. Because of their capacity to see the whole before the parts, gifted learners learn best through concepts. Concept-based curriculum offers students who are CLED, from poverty, and/or twice-exceptional a chance to scaffold learning in a way that best meets their learning preferences and needs.

A concept is an idea that is timeless, abstract, and broad. Two jobs of concepts are to focus the content through a study of topics with skills embedded and to integrate the curriculum. A concept along with an essential understanding serves as the organizing element. Table 1 shares sample universal concepts.

**Essential understandings.** For a concept to be effective, it is necessary to select an essential understanding that focuses on the concept and that can be verified and/or disputed in the course of study. An essential understanding of a concept is a statement that guides the concept and serves as a connector among disciplines. The following are concepts with sample essential understandings:

- *Change*: Change generates change. Change can be positive or negative.
- *Conflict*: Conflict may be natural or man-made. Conflict may be intentional or unintentional.

**TABLE 1**
SAMPLE UNIVERSAL CONCEPTS

| Adaptation | Explorations | Order |
|---|---|---|
| Change | Forces | Patterns |
| Relationships | Conflict | Power |
| Community | Heroism | Structures |
| Interdependence | Independence | Survival |
| Courage | Influences | Traditions |

- *Order*: Order may have repeated patterns. Order may allow for prediction.
- *Patterns*: Patterns have an internal order. Patterns are everywhere.
- *Power*: Power is the ability to influence. Power is always present in some form.
- *Relationships*: Relationships can be natural, forced, or chosen. Relationships can be simple or complex.
- *Structures*: Structures have parts that interrelate. A structure is no stronger than its weakest component part.
- *Systems*: Systems are composed of subsystems and parts. A system may be influenced by other systems.

Once a concept has been chosen and the essential understandings have been determined, the curriculum designer begins the process of organizing and/or integrating the content to be mastered. The following lesson is an example of concept-based learning with the concept of *patterns* on the topic of fairy tales. The suggested essential understanding is *patterns are everywhere*. This lesson integrates social studies content and the lesson of map skills in geography with an English/language arts (ELA) topic of fairy tales and the skill of defining settings. We present this lesson as an example of an effectively differentiated lesson.

Preassessment should always be a part of any unit of study. A discussion of fairy tales will help determine which students have broad or limited knowledge of fairy tales included in the unit of study or fairy tales from other cultures.

# *Fairy Tales*

**Concept:** Patterns

**Skills:** Map skills and setting

**Content:** Social Studies (Geography) and ELA

**Objective:** Illustrate patterns of travel and describe the setting

Students study map skills through fairy tales. Students are asked to find patterns of travel (*setting* from ELA) in self-selected fairy tales. Students select two or three fairy tales for comparison. Students first describe the setting in narrative form and/or with graphics. From the patterns they find, students apply map skills to the development of a map for the travels of the characters in one fairy tale.

## *Activities*

Students explore the concept of *patterns* and essential understanding of *patterns are everywhere* through a choice of fairly tales. Students illustrate through words and graphics in what ways patterns are everywhere in their choice of fairy tale. Through their map skills study, students are asked to verify or invalidate that patterns are everywhere in the fairy tale they select. Students have a choice of products.

How does this lesson make accommodations for underrepresented gifted learners? Examples of product choices:

- Map overlays
- Retelling of fairy tale from a cartographer's point of view
- Explanation of maps using cartographer's terms
- Development of new patterns for retelling/rewriting of fairy tale(s)
- Verbal or written new fairy tale with modern patterns of travel
- Product of student choice with teacher permission

Students from different cultural and/or language backgrounds may share fairy tales from their culture. An extension of this lesson could delve into similarities and differences among various cultures' fairy tales. Students who are twice-exceptional and who have language, verbal/linguistic, and/or visual/spatial abilities or disabilities have the option of oral, written, or spatial representation of products. Students from poverty or any students who have not grown up with exposure to European-based fairy tales may be provided with a set of fairy tales to read to kindergarten students. If language is a difficulty, as a first activity, ask all students to create a play about fairy tales in which Limited English Proficient (LEP) and/or English as a Second Language (ESL) students participate. Another suggestion would be for LEP/ESL students to tell the class a fairy tale in their native language through an interpreter.

**Interdisciplinary content presentation.** Differentiated content may integrate multiple disciplines into work that is self-selected in an area of interest for the student. Kaplan's (1979) work focusing on underrepresented students offers differentiation that connects learning among all disciplines and links to students' learning strengths by operationalizing the terms *depth* and *complexity*. When building on their strengths through differentiation, twice-exceptional and other underrepresented populations' learning needs can more easily be addressed.

Dr. Kaplan developed the dimensions of depth and complexity with key questions and thinking skills through a Javits grant to the Texas Education Agency in 1997. The elements and key questions in Table 2 guide teachers' efforts in development of differentiation for all gifted students, including those who are underrepresented. Through their use with all students, teachers are able to observe behaviors common to *all* gifted learners.

The following unit outline illustrates ways in which the teacher may use the elements of depth and complexity. The notes to teachers indicate the purpose of the activity for underrepresented populations.

**TABLE 2**
ELEMENTS AND KEY QUESTIONS

| Elements That Add Depth to Learning | Key Questions for Elements |
|---|---|
| Language of the Discipline | What terms or words are specific to the work of a professional person? What tools does this professional person use? |
| Details | What are the attributes? What features characterize this? What specific elements define this? What distinguishes this from other things? |
| Patterns | What are the reoccurring events? What elements, events, and ideas are repeated over time? What was the order of events? How can we predict what will come next? |
| Trends | What ongoing factors have influenced this study? What factors have contributed to this study? |
| Unanswered Questions | What is still not understood about this area/topic/study/discipline? What is yet unknown about this area/topic/study/discipline? In what ways is the information incomplete or lacking in explanation? |
| Rules | How is this structured? What are the stated and unstated causes related to the description or explanation of what we are studying? |
| Ethics | What dilemmas or controversies are involved in this area/topic/study/discipline? What elements can be identified that reflect bias, prejudice, and discrimination? |
| Big Ideas | What overarching statement best describes what is being studied? What general statement includes what is being studied? |
| **Elements That Add Complexity to Learning** | **Key Questions for Elements** |
| Over Time | How are the ideas related between the past, present, and future? How are these ideas related within or during a particular time period? How has time affected the information? How and why do things change or remain the same? |
| Different Perspectives | What are the opposing viewpoints? How do different people and characters see this event or situation? |
| Interdisciplinary Relationships | What are common elements among topics from the different disciplines? How does this idea/topic/concept relate to other disciplines? How do topics/ideas from across the disciplines contribute meaning to this idea? |

## Heroes

**Big Idea:** Relationships
**Essential Understanding:** Relationships may be natural, forced, or chosen.

Heroes emerge when people are ready to find them. There must be a venue for the hero, who generally does not emerge if things are going well. There must be some kind of crisis, and then the hero emerges to deal with the problem. In the best stories and fairy tales, after the problem has been solved, the hero disappears back into the mist.

Emergence of the hero may be due to a relationship with a natural phenomenon (e.g., tsunamis, hurricanes, fires), or the hero may be in a situation in which a relationship forces heroism (e.g., wars, family situations, robberies). A third situation is one in which the hero may choose a relationship that allows him or her to become a hero (e.g., care for younger people, as in the Big Brothers/Big Sisters program).

After studying about heroes, students should complete either of the following tasks.

- Describe how your choice of hero became a hero to you and/or others. Use a medium of your preference.
- Create a product using technology-based resources that defines the heroic act as one that was natural, forced, or chosen.

## Product

Students should select one of the following options:

- Create a book about heroes to put in the library of a kindergarten or first-grade class or your school library. Read your book to another class.
- Create a physical representation of a hero and a heroic act. Prepare a presentation to go with your final product.
- Create your own product with your teacher's approval.

## Activities to Guide the Study of Heroes

**Language of the discipline.** Discuss heroes and generate a list of names. Look up the term *hero* and discuss the difference between hero and celebrity. What tools, implements, or devices are used by heroes? (*Teacher's Note*: This research and discussion offers an opportunity for students to present heroes from their culture and environment. Students may be grouped according to similar abilities and/or interests.)

**Details.** What are the attributes of a hero? How do you know someone is a hero? (*Teacher's Note*: Remember that students from poverty often identify with the anti-hero. For a full discussion see Slocumb and Payne, 2000.)

**Patterns.** When do people find heroes? What are the origins of heroes? Can heroism be predicted?

**Trends.** Are heroes always the same? (*Teacher's Note*: Students might talk with their parents and grandparents to determine heroes from previous generations. These heroes could be divided into traditional heroes, such as Superman, Batman, or any of the Marvel Superheroes, or inspirational heroes such as people in the community or people in the military. Students may want to view heroes as fictional or actual. In all cases, students should be instructed to try to identify why this person is a hero. Students may also compare and contrast types of heroes across cultures.)

**Unanswered questions.** Start with a T chart. What do we know about heroes? (*Teacher's Note*: Again, this offers an opportunity for students to present heroes from their own culture and background.) What do we want to know about heroes? (*Teacher's Note*: This provides a base of knowledge, expands the base for all of the students in the group, and provides some opportunity for unanswered questions that lead to independent studies.)

**Rules.** Why do heroes behave as they do? Are there rules for heroes? This is also a place to discuss ethics. Some heroes bring the bad guys in to be tried in court, and others dispense justice on the spot and continue with their winning ways while leaving trail of dead, disabled, and dismembered baddies behind them. What are some ethical principles of the hero? (*Teacher's Note*: Counselors or mentors may help with this activity.)

**Different perspectives.** Think of different cultural heroes, but put a different twist on it—you might also include animals. (*Teacher's Note*: This offers another opportunity to compare and contrast heroes from different cultures.)

**Interdisciplinary relationships.** Connect art, music, and the hero. (*Teacher's Note*: These activities can meet the needs of twice-exceptional students and those from poverty whose strength area is in the arts. For this and other information, visit the following Texas Education Agency websites: http://www.texaspsp.org/toolkit/GT_Teacher_Toolkit.html and http://www.texaspsp.org/all/DepthComplexity.pdf.)

## PROCESS

Differentiating process includes complex, abstract, and/or higher level thinking skills (i.e., critical thinking) and focuses on relevant and open-ended tasks that develop research skills and methods. Berger (1991) suggested that differentiation in process is more demanding in its involvement of higher level and open-ended questioning. When differentiating process, teachers must ensure that basic and advanced content skills are taught through critical and creative thinking. Using a taxonomy of skills is a good way to ensure students are working at high levels of thinking rather than low levels. Students who differ from the majority culture need opportunities to work with advanced content and higher order thinking skills. To facilitate this interaction with advanced content, teachers must scaffold some of the learning activities until the students reach a level of language facility that is commensurate with their intellectual ability. Likewise, students who are twice-exceptional may need additional support through adaptive devices or other modifications to access challenging curriculum.

**Bloom's taxonomy.** One of the most popular taxonomies is Bloom's (1956) taxonomy; however, Anderson and Krathwohl (2001) have provided an updated and expanded version. Most notably, the nouns of the cognitive processes (e.g., knowledge, application) from the older version are now verbs (e.g., remember, apply). Another feature is that *synthesis* is now referred to as *create* and has moved to the highest level, switching places with evaluation (now evaluate). Additionally, the simple one-dimensional stair-step or pyramid graphic generally used to demonstrate the levels of Bloom's has been replaced with a grid to accommodate the new Knowledge Dimension. The Knowledge Dimension categories are factual knowledge, conceptual knowledge, procedural knowledge, and metacognitive knowledge. Thus, one can chart 24 different levels of thinking skills, assuring that the knowledge dimension and the cognitive processes work in partnership.

Table 3 shows the 24 levels of thinking. To show how this works, we have placed a "1" at the intersection of "Understand" and "Procedural Knowledge" as a point of reference for this intersection; thus, a prompt that demonstrates an understanding of a procedure might be: "Use the microscope to demonstrate to your lab partner the correct procedure for focusing both the low and high power lens." To evaluate a student's knowledge of a concept (the intersection of "Evaluate" and "Conceptual Knowledge" where we have placed a "2"), an example prompt might be, "Check the accuracy of your final solution using the concept of supply and demand."

**Frank Williams' Taxonomy of Creative Thinking.** Another taxonomy often used in the classroom is that of Frank Williams (1969). His Taxonomy of Creative Thinking is based on cognitive (fluency, flexibility, originality, elaboration) and affective (risk-taking, complexity, curiosity, imagination) student behaviors. By implementing these dimensions with classroom content, teachers are able to stimulate creative thinking across all curricular areas through their use of particular strategies. For example, in the Heroes unit referenced earlier, the teacher may ask students to brainstorm (fluency, imagination) all of the attributes of a hero as a preliminary activity before they actually create their own myth.

Some students who are twice-exceptional, come from poverty, or come from other cultures may find it easier to demonstrate mastery of a topic through creative thinking. Creativity in the classroom can be supported and enhanced through the purposeful introduction of other strategies such as Creative Problem Solving (McIntosh & Meacham, 1992), SCAMPER (Eberle, 2008), synectics (Gordon, 1971), and attribute listing.

Used in tandem, both Bloom's Revised taxonomy (Anderson & Krathwohl, 2001) and Williams's (1969) taxonomy may serve to develop deep levels of thinking and learning in students who are CLED, of poverty, or have other exceptionalities. These taxonomies provide a way to characterize the processes used for students to practice and make sense

**TABLE 3**
NEW LEVELS OF BLOOM'S TAXONOMY

| Cognitive Processes → / Knowledge Dimension ↓ | Remember | Understand | Apply | Analyze | Evaluate | Create |
|---|---|---|---|---|---|---|
| Factual Knowledge | | | | | | |
| Conceptual Knowledge | | | | | 2 | |
| Procedural Knowledge | | 1 | | | | |
| Metacognitive Knowledge | | | | | | |

out of the content. Furthermore, these tools assist teachers in preparing a high-quality curriculum using effective instructional practices that encourage students to develop their productive, complex, abstract, and/or higher level thinking skills. When underrepresented learners with gifts and talents approach learning through process differentiation strategies appropriate to their learning strengths, they may be better able to demonstrate knowledge, skills, and understanding. For example, when students from underrepresented populations miss school due to a move from one location to another or a family crisis, they often miss skills taught during their absence. Rather than providing drill-and-skill worksheets to catch them up on missed work, gifted students who are from the target populations may be given an opportunity to learn the missed material through a higher order thinking activity that involves critical and creative thinking.

## PRODUCT

Product differentiation promotes product development that is based on the creation of unique ideas. Products should exemplify learning that challenges current best thinking, creates new ideas, and uses new techniques and materials. They may also reflect the students' favored learning preference or challenge students to experiment with less favored preferences in order to expand their thinking and skills. Products reveal best thinking that synthesizes and evaluates information and includes students' self-evaluations; products must include new techniques, materials, and forms. Students from underserved populations may demonstrate previously untapped skills when products are differentiated. Rather than requiring students to show their knowledge through a written test or research paper, students may excel in areas where they have previously struggled with a choice of product. For example, a child may demonstrate knowledge of the parts of a plant cell through a project involving traditional folk embroidery or the properties of sound through the building of an instrument native to the child's culture. Rubrics should always accompany these projects so students know the criteria necessary for constructing a project at an expert level.

Sample criteria for quality products suggested by the Texas Education Agency's (2010) Texas Performance Standards Project (TPSP) incorporate critical attributes of learning while providing opportunities for students to develop professional quality products. TPSP offers nine dimensions of product scoring that encompasses a variety of skills and abilities particular to gifted learners:

- *Knowledge and skills*: the sum of what has been learned related to the topic of study.
- *Innovation and application*: using knowledge and skills in creative ways as evidenced through a product.
- *Analysis and synthesis*: using thinking processes to break topics into parts and create a new whole.
- *Ethics/unanswered questions*: applying rules of conduct that govern a field of study, yet lacking consensus among professionals in the named field; asking questions about a field of study that have not been previously asked or answered.
- *Multiple perspectives*: examining an issue from more than one point of view, especially that of the student.
- *Methodology and use of resources*: using principles, procedures, practices, and references from a selected field of study.
- *Communication*: conveying learning through written, spoken, and technological means.
- *Relevance and significance*: expressing the potential of the product on the field of study and others interested in the research and product.
- *Professional quality work*: demonstrating skills and knowledge through a product that is of quality comparable to that of a professional working in the field of study (Texas Education Agency, 2006).

A full explanation of each criterion and rubrics for evaluation may be found at the Texas Education Agency's website for TPSP (http://www.texaspsp.org).

Learners who are twice-exceptional and from other underrepresented populations are able to express their learning through products that match their learning strengths. Although these are good guidelines for all students, they are vital for those who are gifted but have other factors in operation that may interfere with displaying their talents to their full capabilities. As their skills increase, they can expand their repertoire of products that communicate learning in other ways.

A note of caution for assigning projects and products to gifted students from poverty or those who may have other extenuating circumstances at home: Teachers need to recognize that the students may lack financial and, often, emotional resources to complete extensive projects. When there is not money for special items required of a project or an adult willing or able to support any type of production at home, gifted students in poverty may avoid the project altogether. Teachers may need to assist by providing materials and support at school rather than having the project completed at home. In addition to a lack of resources, the need for these students to connect to their current, concrete world is necessary for product development. For example, when studying chaos versus order in the context of war, students from poverty may first need to create a product that reflects order versus chaos in their neighborhood or school and then compare and contrast that with the context of war.

## AFFECT

Differentiation through the affective area guides the gifted as they understand their learning preferences, their motivations for learning, and their giftedness. In the case of those who are twice-exceptional, from poverty, and/or from other cultures, issues that stem from these differences add another layer to understanding affective needs. It is vital that teachers and other school personnel understand the interactions of the various layers. According to Carol Tomlinson (2008), "Most of the affective snares bright kids encounter are a result of a negative interaction of two variables: brightness and basic human need" (p. 6).

The asynchronous development typical of gifted students, being mature in one area and immature in another, brings with it possible additional problems. Teachers may expect the same level of maturity in the affective arena that the child shows in academics. Teachers often overlook the fact that a highly verbal second grader may have the social immaturity of a much younger child. Students who are gifted and from underserved populations bring to the table issues particular to their own situation. As with any other child, these students need to feel safe physically and emotionally in the classroom setting. Teachers must provide choice and challenge while at the same time providing a safety net to encourage students to stay in the struggle to meet the challenge. As Tomlinson (2008) put it, "A great teacher continues to ask the question, 'What can I do to make certain that each student in this classroom feels safe, valued, accepted, and challenged?'" (p. 6).

Rance-Roney (2004) identified several affective issues that must be addressed with students who are culturally and linguistically diverse. One issue that may be totally overlooked is the position these students may have held in their family because of their exceptional academic gifts and talents in their home country. Often schools do not consider these students' academic talent when placing them in classrooms; the focus instead is on their lack of facility in the English language. When these students are automatically placed in lower level classes, the loss of their status in their previous school as well as in their family may be devastating. Another issue is that of learning preferences and strengths. Students who are culturally and linguistically diverse as well as students from poverty and twice-exceptional students may have very different learning preferences and strengths than other students in the classroom. Teachers must be sure to allow students a variety of ways to show understanding to account for these different strengths and preferences; teachers must also be aware of their own tendencies toward a single way of presenting material. Delivering the content through a variety of modes, as well as allowing multiple ways to show understanding, is critical to meeting the affective needs of these students.

Knowledge of self is another facet of affect in the classroom. Students must have opportunities to learn about themselves as learners and the part that their giftedness plays in their lives. Teachers must assist students in understanding that more than their giftedness defines them. When students tie their self-worth to their classroom performance, the opportunity for psychosocial problems occurs. One way to assist students in understanding their strengths and areas for improvement is through self-evaluations. A requirement of a final product could have a self-evaluation component. Students could be asked to assess their effort, what they learned, and how they might improve their project. Providing a rubric along with an assignment allows students to score themselves against a benchmark. Self-evaluation combined with rubric evaluations and other standardized instructions allow the students to grow intellectually and personally. Peer evaluations permit students to learn how to give and receive constructive feedback and assess others' strengths that may be different from their own. All of these tools provide students with an opportunity to create a realistic snapshot of their abilities at a particular point in time. Affective skills such as these are essential components of differentiation for this population of gifted students. Students' understanding of their own abilities and appreciation of other students' skills are critical ingredients in the mixture that is the underrepresented student who is gifted. Self-understanding will elicit quality self-appraisal through criterion-referenced or standardized measures.

In the case of gifted students from poverty, teachers need to be cognizant that they may see themselves in a plural context because of the possibility of a number of people living together in small quarters. Lack of physical space may create an atmosphere of chaos in which each person is vying for attention and space. These factors create difficulty for independent study for students from poverty (see Slocumb & Payne, 2000).

With students who are twice-exceptional, self-identity is also an issue. Students may see themselves in light of their other exceptionality rather than as gifted. For example, a student may see herself as someone who is visually impaired and in need of many accommodations, totally discounting that accommodations must also be in place to support her gifts and talents. Teachers and aides may be so intent on accommodating the visual impairment that they neglect to modify the curriculum to provide depth and challenge.

In summary, affective needs of the gifted are manifest in a variety of ways. Teachers must acknowledge that gifted students develop asynchronously, see themselves through a loss of status when entering a school without knowledge of the school's home language, illustrate learning through a learning preference beyond that of the majority of students, see their self-worth in terms of their exceptionality while ignoring learning strengths, or lack practice with working alone in independent study. This diversity within affective needs is as vital to school success for the twice-exceptional learner as are content acquisition, process development, and product illustration of learning.

## LEARNING ENVIRONMENT

Learning environment refers to the physical and mental area provided for underrepresented gifted students' learning and production. According to Berger (1991),

> Gifted students learn best in a receptive, nonjudgmental, student-centered environment that encourages inquiry and independence, includes a wide variety of materials, provides some physical movement, is generally complex, and connects the school experience with the greater world. . . . it is essential that the teacher establish a climate that encourages them to question, exercise independence, and use their creativity in order to be all that they can be. (p. 2)

For appropriate differentiation to occur, the learning environment is equal in importance to content, process, product, and affect for students who are gifted and from underrepresented populations. Clearly, the teacher is a crucial factor in setting the learning environment stage to ensure success for students from underrepresented populations. Fertig (2006) summarized characteristics of teachers from an online questionnaire. According to the questionnaire,

> effective teachers of the gifted have the following characteristics:
> - high degree of intelligence, intellectual honesty;
> - expertise in a specific intellectual or talent area (mathematics, writing, etc.);
> - self-directed in own learning, with a love for new, advanced knowledge;
> - equanimity, level-headedness, emotional stability;
> - a genuine interest in, liking of gifted learners;
> - recognition of the importance of intellectual development;
> - strong belief in individual differences and individualization; and
> - highly developed teaching skills and knowledge.

Student responses suggest effective teachers of the gifted need to:

- be patient,
- have a sense of humor,
- move quickly through material,
- treat each student as an individual,
- avoid being a "sage on the stage" all the time, and
- consistently give "accurate" feedback. (Fertig, 2006, para. 2–3)

In *Selective Students' Views of the Essential Characteristics of Effective Teachers*, Vialle and Quigley (2002) found that characteristics can be grouped into three themes: teachers' knowledge and skills, teaching and classroom management style, and interpersonal qualities. In their synthesis, they found that characteristics include:

- having insights into the cognitive, social, and emotional needs of gifted students;
- having skills in differentiating the curriculum for gifted students;
- employing strategies that encourage higher level thinking;
- encouraging students to be independent learners;
- providing student-centered learning opportunities;
- acting as a facilitator or "guide on the side";
- creating a nonthreatening learning environment;
- being well organized;
- possessing in-depth knowledge of subject matter;
- having broad interests, often literary and cultural;
- having above-average intelligence;
- being a lifelong learner;
- thinking creatively;
- possessing excellent communication skills;
- being willing to make mistakes;
- possessing a sense of humor; and
- being enthusiastic.

The teacher who creates the appropriate differentiated environment for the underrepresented gifted student is one who recognizes a home environment, that all cultural experiences the student brings to the class

**TABLE 4**
VALUE SYSTEMS

| Poverty | Middle Class | Wealth |
|---------|--------------|--------|
| Survival | Work | Political connections |
| Relationships | Achievement | Financial connections |
| Entertainment | Material security | Social connections |

must be connected with the school environment, and the special learning needs of the twice-exceptional learner. These lists can guide administrators in the hiring process and aid parents in determining the best fit for their gifted student.

# THE ROLE OF POVERTY

Gifted students of poverty frequently do not understand the middle-class rules of school that are generally essential to school success. Students from poverty are often denied access to high-quality curriculum and instruction due to a mismatch between the rules of poverty and that of the school's dominant culture (the middle class). As such, these students may not even get into the talent pool, much less the gifted program. For example, Payne (2005) noted differences in the value systems among the three socioeconomic levels in Table 4.

According to Slocumb and Payne (2000), three issues cloud giftedness in students of poverty:

- *Lack of linear orientation:* This lack of linear orientation is related to differing perception of time between children of poverty and those of middle class. The middle class is future- and goal-oriented because of the values of work and achievement. Because children of poverty are focused on survival, future thinking and goal setting are not required. When students of poverty rely on fate to deliver needs, goal setting is a foreign concept.
- *Difficulty in abstracting:* Even though gifted students are described as conceptual thinkers, students from poverty are often limited by their concrete surroundings being based in the senses and

emotion. They do not hear adults discussing savings accounts and future plans that are abstract; they do hear adults talking about the present and current issues that contribute to survival. Because of their lack of exposure to abstract thought, gifted students from poverty may have difficulty with abstract concepts.

- *Avoidance of academic rigor.* Some adults from low-income backgrounds may not be comfortable with the school taking a place of importance in their children's lives. In many cases, adults in poverty sometimes feel that school should be another form of entertainment. That fact, coupled with the importance of entertainment in the culture of poverty, creates an atmosphere that does not lend itself to a need for academic rigor. Gifted children in poverty may seem to avoid academic rigor not only because of this lack of adult support, but also because they lack the financial and emotional resources to complete required class work.

These three factors offer insight into differences between the school's middle-class values and those that gifted students in poverty bring to school with them. This mismatch creates a need for educators to find more appropriate opportunities and scaffolding for this population.

# THE ROLE OF MULTICULTURALISM

Ford, Howard, Harris, and Tyson (2000), leading researchers on the subject of multiculturalism for gifted students, posed these questions to educators:

- What is "culture" and how does it affect teaching and learning?
- What are my minority students interested in learning?
- What teaching strategies are culturally congruent and responsive? (p. 421)

They continued:

In culturally responsive classrooms: students are placed at the center of teaching and learning. . . . multicultural education is a central component of the curriculum; . . . All students, regardless of their racial and cultural background, learn from a nonbiased curriculum. (Ford et al., 2000, pp. 409, 411)

Borland (2004) added to this perspective, noting that "Such a curriculum [multicultural] need not be terribly elaborate. We employ a diagnostic-prescriptive model, along with some interdisciplinary enrichment, work on thinking skills, and help developing academic 'meta-skills,' . . . and maintain a multicultural perspective" (p. 22). Underrepresented students benefit from a differentiated curriculum that embraces their culture and that of *all* students in their environment.

Differentiation of content, process, product, and learning environment is an important aspect of gifted education; it is equally important in the education of students who are culturally, linguistically, economically, and ethnically diverse as well as for twice-exceptional students. Imagine being one of these students and only reading about White middleclass students with no disabilities; all students deserve to see themselves reflected in what they learn in school. When differentiating for gifted students who are diverse, the following practices should be evident:

- Content, including materials and resources, has a definite multicultural focus.
- Strategies and teaching style are closely matched to the learning preferences of the students, giving thoughtful and purposeful consideration to students' backgrounds and characteristics.
- Products address issues and problems that have a multicultural focus.
- The learning environment is created to honor diversity; all individuals are respected and valued.
- Affective needs of diverse students are understood and are reflected in the curriculum, learning environment, and all others aspects of learning (Ford, 2004, p. 77).

To be certain that our exceptional and diverse gifted students have their unique affective and learning needs addressed, teachers must be constantly vigilant that modifications to meet their needs are determined not only through the gifted lens, but also through the lens of diversity.

# SUMMARY

In this chapter, we have focused on differentiation and the components that are necessary for effective differentiation to take place. We looked at the various aspects of instruction and environment that could be differentiated to meet the needs of underserved populations and offered some examples of appropriately differentiated activities. We also underscored poverty and multiculturalism, two factors that must be considered for effective differentiation to occur for students with gifts and talents from underserved populations.

# CHAPTER 3

# Acceleration

Acceleration is a way to speed up the pace at which learning is occurring. There are many forms of acceleration, but some common ways are through compacting the material, subject skipping, and grade skipping. Acceleration is the subject of the research in *A Nation Deceived: How Schools Hold Back America's Brightest Students* (Colangelo, Assouline, & Gross, 2004). This report, commissioned by the Templeton Foundation and developed at the Connie Belin and Jacqueline N. Blank International Center for Gifted Education and Talent Development, offered the following examples of statements supporting acceleration:

- Acceleration is the most effective curriculum intervention for gifted children.
- Testing, especially above-level testing (using tests developed for older students), is highly effective in identifying students who would benefit from acceleration.
- Entering school early is an excellent option for some gifted students both academically and socially. High ability young children who enroll early generally settle in smoothly with their older classmates.
- Gifted students entering college early experience both short-term and long-term academic success, leading to long-term occupational success and personal satisfaction.
- Many alternatives to full-time early college entrance are available for bright high school students who prefer to stay with age-peers.

These include dual enrollment in high school and college, distance education, and summer programs. Advanced Placement (AP) is the best large-scale option for bright students who want to take college-level courses in high school.

- Radical acceleration (acceleration by two or more years) is effective academically and socially for highly gifted students.
- Educational equity does not mean educational sameness. Equity respects individual differences in readiness to learn and recognizes the value of each student.
- The key question for educators is not *whether* to accelerate a gifted learner but rather *how*. (Colangelo et al., 2004, p. 2)

We will discuss content-based acceleration, grade-based acceleration, pacing, and curriculum compacting below, but for a full discussion of all forms of acceleration see Colangelo et al. (2004).

# CONTENT-BASED ACCELERATION

Two categories of acceleration described by the members of the National Work Group on Acceleration (Colangelo et al., 2010) are content-based and grade-based. Content-based acceleration is defined in two ways:

- advanced skills or understandings before the expected age or grade level while remaining with age and grade peers and
- higher grade-level instruction in the regular classroom in lieu of grade-level instruction (Colangelo et al., 2010, p. 184).

Colangelo et al. (2010) listed the following as examples of content-based acceleration:

- *Single subject acceleration*: Students are given opportunities to move beyond their age-mates in a subject area of strength (e.g., a third-grade student may attend sixth-grade math class, but remain with third-grade peers for all other subjects).
- *Curriculum compacting*: This is a practice that preassesses students to free them from the redundancy of learning content they

already know and provides time to master content in areas of learning needs.

- *Dual enrollment*: Students may be enrolled in a class on a high school or college campus that earns both high school and college credit.
- *Credit-by-exam or prior experience*: This is a method in which a student may receive credit for a subject or course or accelerate through a grade by taking one or more exams.
- *Advanced Placement coursework*: Coursework that is delivered in a College Board sanctioned class that is designated as Advanced Placement.
- *International Baccalaureate program*: Students may be enrolled in an International Baccalaureate Primary Years Programme (grades K–5), Middle Years Programme (grades 6–10), or Diploma/ Certificate Programme (grades 11–12).

# GRADE-BASED ACCELERATION

Grade-based acceleration is often referred to as *grade skipping*, in which students spend fewer years in the K–12 system unless they take early entrance to kindergarten as an option and skip no other grades. Examples of grade-based acceleration are "early entrance to school, whole-grade acceleration . . ., grade telescoping, and early entrance to college" (Colangelo et al., 2010, p. 186). There are many beliefs and myths surrounding grade-based acceleration, such as: "The student will have social and emotional problems," "The student will be upset when others begin driving and she isn't old enough yet," and "The student's mind is not ready to handle advanced content." One way to allay some of these fears is to share the acceleration research that discounts these beliefs with both school faculty and parents. Another option is to use an instrument to determine whether or not acceleration is an appropriate option.

# ASSESSING FOR ACCELERATION OPPORTUNITIES

Often students from underrepresented populations are not considered for acceleration. Many of these students enter school without skill sets and knowledge that other students may have acquired prior to starting school. Hence, these students may be considered low performers or placed in remedial courses when in fact they are bright students who have not been previously exposed to the material. Providing alternative assessment opportunities or embedded assessments may allow teachers to have a clearer portrait of the learning strengths of these students. When interpreting results from standardized tests, teachers need to remember to look at students from underrepresented populations in relation to their reference groups (i.e., students from the same environment and/or with similar experiences).

The Iowa Acceleration Scale (Assouline, Colangelo, Lupkowski-Shoplik, Forstadt, & Lipscomb, 2003) is an excellent tool to use in determining whether either content-based or grade-based acceleration is an appropriate choice for a student. By gathering data and answering a series of questions, the user can make an objective decision about the possibility of acceleration as a viable choice for a particular student. There are periodic junctures where answers to the questions determine whether or not the next section of the scale should be completed. Once the scale is completed, a norms table provides a guide for determining the candidate's suitability for acceleration.

# PACE OF LEARNING

Quite often, gifted students will need to have the pace of their studies changed for challenge to continue. Pacing is a form of acceleration that echoes the types discussed above. Teachers may change the pace of the material to cover twice as much material in half the time, for example. This accommodation is based on the ability of certain students to take in knowledge at a faster rate, understand it, and move to the next, more difficult concept in a shorter period of time. When this process involves covering several grade levels in a shorter period of time, it is called grade telescoping. For example, a group of fifth-grade students who have been identified as highly gifted in math may cover fifth-, sixth-, and seventh-grade math in one year, which allows them to move on to algebra in the sixth grade.

# CURRICULUM COMPACTING

Renzulli and Reis (2004) defined curriculum compacting as:

an instructional technique that is specifically designed to make appropriate curricular adjustments for students in any curricular area and at any grade level. Essentially, the procedure involves (1) defining the goals and outcomes of a particular unit or block of instruction, (2) determining and documenting the students who have already mastered most or all of a specified set of learning outcomes, and (3) providing replacement strategies for material already mastered through the use of instructional options that enable a more challenging, interesting, and productive use of the student's time. (p. 91)

Through this instructional technique, the teacher assesses students prior to teaching a new skill or new content to determine what the student does and does not know and designs alternative experiences that will replace those activities designed for content already mastered. Curriculum compacting streamlines and modifies grade-level curriculum by eliminating material that students have previously learned. By eliminating material previously learned, the teacher can provide new materials that challenge students and offer time for differentiated enrichment or acceleration activities to students who demonstrate high levels of achievement. Curriculum compacting gives the student the opportunity to develop in ways that accommodate learning needs and provides teachers the chance to create learning experiences of greater depth, complexity, and breadth.

There are two types of compacting: basic skills and content. Basic skills compacting involves tasks that students routinely complete in drill and practice sessions. Examples are spelling words, math computations, and basic grammar skills in English language arts. Preassessment can determine the students' level of expertise with basic skills.

The second type of curriculum compacting relates to content. Core content areas can be compacted as can strands within each content (e.g., through concepts and essential understandings). Often students know a great deal about the subject or can learn it very quickly through reading or practice that is based on higher order thinking. Curriculum compacting for students who are from underrepresented populations frees them from the redundancy of learning content they already know and gives them the time to master content in areas of learning needs.

Records need to be kept so that teachers, students, and other stakeholders are aware of what students know, understand, and are able to do, as well as what material has been compacted and the nature of the alternative assignments. A streamlined and simplified version of the original Compactor designed by Reis and Renzulli (2004) can easily be created (see Figure 1). In the first column, *Name It*, the teacher lists the work that is to be covered (e.g., three-dimensional geometric objects). In the second column, *Prove It*, data that demonstrate a strong understanding of the concept are listed (e.g., the score on the pretest, other assessment information). In the third column, *Change It*, the alternate area of study and the activities that the student will complete are listed (e.g., the study of fractals and fractional dimensions). Figure 1 depicts a streamlined Compactor for Maria, a sixth-grade student in mathematics.

When students are accelerated through grade or subject skipping, they are generally placed at the grade or subject level that provides a challenge commensurate with their ability. In most cases, they simply study the topic at the new level and at the pace already set. When curriculum is compacted so that students only cover the portions that they have not yet mastered, they generally remain in the class with their age-mates but instructional time is then freed for them to pursue the topic in more depth or study a related topic. Enrichment is often chosen by the teacher as a means to supplement the content being covered; thus, compacting connects acceleration and enrichment.

| Name It | Prove It | Change It |
|---------|----------|-----------|
| General education curriculum: three-dimensional geometric shapes (cube, sphere, rectangular prism, pyramid) | Maria received 98% on the pretest for this topic. She has been identified as gifted in mathematics using the TOMAGS and the ITBS Math Application section out-of-level; she scored in the highest range on the Fall NWEA MAP in math. | Maria will begin her study of fractals by using materials gathered by the teacher including books, websites, videos, and fractal-generating software. The teacher and Maria will have twice-weekly conferences to monitor progress. Maria will demonstrate what she has learned through a multimedia presentation to the class, including examples of fractals in other cultures. Her project will introduce others to the world of fractals; she will also produce an original fractal. |

*Figure 1.* Maria's Compactor.

# SUMMARY

In this chapter, we introduced and discussed several forms of acceleration. We explained how these forms can allow gifted learners from underserved populations to have access to material at a faster pace or at a higher level of complexity. We identified some factors that often limit these students' access to acceleration as a viable option. When choosing acceleration options for students from underserved populations, it is critical to focus on student strengths.

# CHAPTER 4

# Enrichment

Another effective practice is enrichment. Generally, enrichment activities allow students who have mastered the grade-level material to study the topic in more depth or breadth or at a more complex level while other students needing more practice continue to work with the general education or grade-level curriculum. At a time when there is an emphasis on basic skills and standards, the general education curriculum generally lacks the challenge that students who are gifted need to allow them to learn something new every day. If acceleration is not a viable option, then enrichment may address the chasm between what the gifted student needs and what the general curriculum has to offer.

There are some types of gifted programs that emphasize enrichment. One such model is the Schoolwide Enrichment Model (see Renzulli & Reis, 1997, for a full discussion), based on the idea of creative productivity. When schools have gifted programs that involve students being pulled out of class to go to a resource room to meet with a teacher who provides enrichment materials, this model is one that is often used. During tight economic times, services for students who are gifted are often provided sporadically in the general education classroom when the teacher has time to work with these students. For our purposes, we will define enrichment as "modifications a teacher makes to go above and beyond the regular curriculum for a student or cluster of students who need advanced learning opportunities" (Roberts, 2005, p. 6).

To be clear, enrichment for the sake of providing fun activities for those who have finished their work or who already understand the material being presented is not what we are advocating. Although the enrichment may be in content, process, or product, substantial content must be involved. Simply having students engage in an exciting project such as making a piñata is best situated within a discussion of cultures whose celebrations include piñatas, the science involved in making papier-mâché, or the origins of papier-mâché. Hands-on learning necessitates simultaneous minds-on learning.

Enrichment that is tied directly to the curriculum is advantageous because the learning is sequenced, allowing the new information to be connected to that previously learned in addition to being able to progress in a logical manner (Schiever & Maker, 2003). The content remains organized around what students should know, understand, and be able to do while extending the foundations to include connections to other topics and disciplines. Research on ability groups by Kulik (1992) supports the notion of enrichment; there were marked differences among groups when the curriculum was adjusted to reflect the performance level of the students. Along those same lines, Rogers (1991) found an effect size of .65 when students were grouped by ability in a pull-out program using a curriculum extension approach.

For students who are from underrepresented populations, enrichment is an important option. Many of these students may come from backgrounds where there is no money or no opportunity for personal or academic enrichment. Even a simple trip to the zoo may not be feasible. For some of these students, the issue is access; for others, it is finances; and for some, it is both. By providing opportunities for enrichment in the classroom, the teacher may be able to fill an intellectual and/or experiential void. Exposure to enrichment material nurtures the talents of these students and provides opportunities for future talent development.

Inspecting material gathered as part of the students' learning profiles coupled with information about their interests in a particular area can be the basis for developing enrichment activities. Providing opportunities to connect to the cultural, linguistic, and ethnic strengths of the child is just as critical as providing the necessary scaffolding academically. For example, perhaps a student for whom English is a second language has a favorite author who writes in her native language. The student could compare and contrast this author's style with the author of a current book she is reading in language arts class. This provides the student practice with higher level thinking skills in her native language and in English to produce a written piece in her new language.

Following is a sample lesson that could be used for whole-class or small-group enrichment. In Appendix A, we have also included an enrichment unit that is multicultural in focus and provides multiple opportunities to address student strengths.

## *Dichotomous Keys/Taxonomies*

**Grade Level:** K–12
**Subject:** Science
**Topic:** Dichotomous Keys/Taxonomies
**Standards Addressed:**

- National Science Teaching Standard A: Teachers of science plan an inquiry-based science program for their students.
- National Science Education Content Standard A: As a result of activities in grades K–12, all students should develop abilities necessary to do scientific inquiry and understandings about scientific inquiry.
- National Association for Gifted Children Pre-K–Grade 12 Gifted Programming Standard 3: Curriculum Planning and Instruction: 3.4. Instructional Strategies. Students with gifts and talents become independent investigators.

**Overarching Theme:** Systems
**Subtopic:** Classification Systems
**Essential Understanding:** Scientists put similar things into groups to better understand the similarities and differences among them.
**Essential Questions:**

- How do we determine how to group particular organisms?
- What kinds of attributes are important when classifying organisms?
- How do scientists decide where to place an unknown organism?
- What advantages are there to having a classification system?

Table 5 may be used to plot the levels of essential questions.

Students should *know*:
- Vocabulary: classification, taxonomy, dichotomous, attribute
- Every organism receives two names, a genus and a species. These names are Latin or Greek in origin.

Students should *understand*:
- Scientists use dichotomous keys to identify to which kingdom, phylum, class, and so forth an organism belongs.

Students should be able to *do*:
- Classify a given set of objects.
- Make a dichotomous key.
- Use a dichotomous key.
- Create names for unknown species.

## Background

Prior to this lesson, students have had some practice in naming attributes of a set of items and placing the items into similar groups. They understand the scientific processes of observation and gathering data.

### Activity 1

This is at the concrete level. The cards can be made from pictures, stamps, or stickers. The number and type of cards used can be differentiated according to students' readiness levels. For example, for younger children, familiar animals might be used. However, this activity uses bacteria cards, which are appropriate for upper elementary, middle, and high school levels. Pictures of bacteria may be found on the Internet or in scientific catalogs.

1. Introduce the activity with an object that is familiar (e.g., cube). Make a short dichotomous key that could be used to demonstrate how to separate this object from others. Figure 2 shares part of a

**TABLE 5**
CHART USED TO PLOT THE LEVELS OF ESSENTIAL QUESTIONS

| Cognitive Processes ⇨ / Knowledge Dimension ⇩ | Remember | Understand | Apply | Analyze | Evaluate | Create |
|---|---|---|---|---|---|---|
| Factual Knowledge | | | | | | |
| Conceptual Knowledge | | | | | | |
| Procedural Knowledge | | | | | | |
| Metacognitive Knowledge | | | | | | |

| 1a | Object is three-dimensional | Go to 2a |
|----|------------------------------|----------|
| 1b | Object is not three-dimensional | Go to 2b |
| 2a | Object has more than four equal sides | Object is a cube |
| 2b | Object does not have more than four equal sides | Object is a square |

*Figure 2.* Dichotomous key example.

longer key that differentiates 2- and 3-dimensional objects. Show the students the key and explain its use.

2. Distribute the cards the students will use and the appropriate dichotomous key.

3. Have the students use the key to classify all of the organisms in their set. Each organism should have a unique identity.

4. Check to be sure all students have classified the organisms correctly.

5. For students who have a good understanding of using the key and who were successful with the activity, move to Activity 2. For those who struggled with the activity, modify it by using fewer cards and have them repeat the activity.

## Activity 2

This activity is more abstract. Students are given a set of objects to classify and then make their own dichotomous key for their organisms. At this point, you may use actual specimens (e.g., seashells). Alternatively, you may use inanimate objects for more abstractness, such as snack chips. With actual specimens, students will need to research the scientific names of the organisms. With inanimate objects, students may make up names, but they still must use the Latin/Greek nomenclature. Note that both names are italicized and that the genus is capitalized and the species is lowercase. For example, *Potato chipis alba* might be a white potato chip, where "Potato chipis" is the genus, and "alba" is the species. Other options are peanuts, pasta, buttons, stuffed animals, "found objects," and so forth. Once students have constructed their dichotomous key, have them exchange their sets of objects and keys to see if other students can use the key to correctly classify the objects. Students may want to bring in a collection of objects that represents their culture, interest, or other meaningful sets. For students who need some scaffolding, supply a framework for sorting the items into groups first (see Figure 3, which is a framework for classifying four items).

Below are directions for the students with sample answers in parentheses:
1. Look at the entire set of objects. What is common to all of the objects? (They are all seashells; they are all buttons.)
2. Try to sort the objects into two groups based on an attribute. For example, you choose to organize a set of six buttons into red and not red. Notice that we don't name the two groups by separate names, such as red and black. We always use the name of the attribute and the other items are "not" that attribute.
3. Write down the attribute. This will be the first section of your key.
4. Next, choose to work with only one of the groups, for example, the red group. Consider all of the members of the red group and break that group into two groups based on an attribute, such as buttonholes and no buttonholes. Write down that attribute for your next section.
5. Continue until you have each red button classified into its own unique group. Keep track of the attributes you used.
6. Repeat Steps 4 and 5 with the not red group.
7. Look at the attributes you wrote and design your key so that by using the key, anyone could classify each unique button.
8. Here is an example of a classification key for three buttons, a red one with buttonholes, a blue one with buttonholes, and a red one without buttonholes:

| 1a | Button has button holes | Go to 2 |
|----|-------------------------|---------|
| 1b | Button does not have button holes | Red button, no buttonholes |
| 2a | Button is red | Red button with buttonholes |
| 2b | Button is not red | Blue button with buttonholes |

9. Double check to be sure all of your items have been uniquely classified.

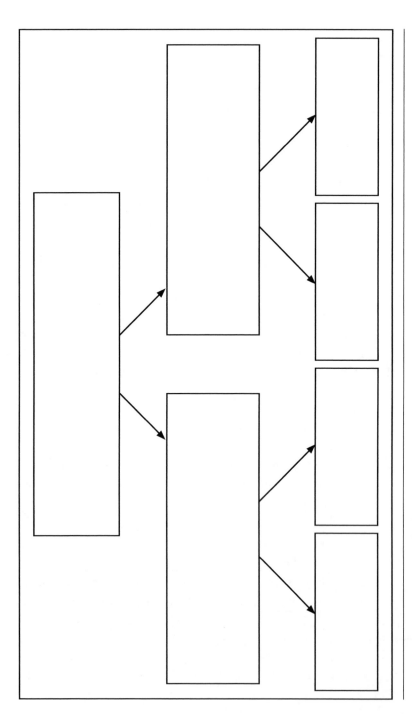

*Figure 3.* Classification framework for four items.

## *Assessment*

Here are two examples of assessments that you can use with this lesson. First, you can provide students with a set of objects not previously used (pictures of objects may also be used) and have students make a dichotomous key. Check the key for accuracy. Second, you can provide students with a prepared dichotomous key and a set of objects. Have students identify the objects in each set. Check for accuracy. Initiate a class discussion using the Essential Questions.

## *Scientist Extension*

For those who want to delve deeper into the topic of scientific nomenclature and dichotomous keys, here are two scientists whose work was in those areas:

- Alice Eastwood: a famous American botanist who was curator of botany at the California Academy of Science.
- Carl Linnaeus: a Swedish naturalist who developed binomial nomenclature, the system of naming, ranking, and classifying organisms.

# OUT-OF-SCHOOL ENRICHMENT OPPORTUNITIES

It should be noted that other enrichment opportunities include academic teams, content-based clubs and organizations, afterschool programs, and Saturday and summer programs. Typically, these are not easily accessible to students who are from poverty; culturally, linguistically, and ethnically diverse; or who are twice-exceptional. School leaders must take a close look at who is attending these programs and, if these students are underrepresented, find ways for them to participate. For example, students whose families do not have a reliable means of transportation may not be able to get their children to Saturday programs. Using the school's buses may solve this problem. Those who work and must leave their children in the care of others may not be able to transport their children to summer programs. Providing all-day programs at the school could potentially solve this problem. Programs that charge a fee for attending may be too expensive for some. Defraying the expense of attending for those not able to pay would allow them to participate. Opportunities are not equal when the nature of the program makes it inaccessible to some who qualify for the services.

The Suggested Resources section of this book provides information on various programs that are available nationwide. Locally, a good place to start is to contact a nearby college or university to inquire if there are programs offered in an area of interest for K–12 students.

# SUMMARY

In this chapter, we have defined enrichment and identified ways to use it appropriately with gifted learners from underserved populations. We looked at in-school and out-of-school enrichment opportunities and provided some cautions about making sure all students have equal access to these opportunities. In addition, we urge you to look at the Suggested Resources section for some excellent articles and websites that address enrichment. Be sure to also look at the sample enrichment unit included in Appendix A.

# CHAPTER 5

# Recommendations

In this book, we have presented three effective practices for learners with gifts and talents who come from underserved populations. In each chapter, we have discussed the particular practice, provided examples, and indicated how the practice can impact our target learners. We have attempted to highlight areas of concern and potential issues that are often overlooked when working with these students. In this section, we offer some suggestions for administrators, counselors, teachers, and parents that we hope will assist them in meeting the needs of these students.

## ADMINISTRATORS

- Inspect your school's plan for identifying gifted students. Be sure you have reliable and valid instruments and appropriate practices for identifying students who are twice-exceptional; culturally, linguistically, and ethnically diverse; and those from poverty. In many cases, they must be identified to receive services.
- Develop an acceleration policy. Banish myths surrounding acceleration by providing appropriate research to counselors, educators, and parents. Without a policy, acceleration may not be seen as a viable option for gifted students.
- Provide professional development opportunities addressing the

identification and needs of students from underserved populations as well as effective practices for meeting those needs.
- Support staff members who are willing to engage in effective practices for these students.
- Provide financial support so that appropriate materials may be purchased to allow effective practices to be implemented.

# COUNSELORS

- Assist in identifying students from underserved populations who may potentially be gifted students.
- Seek appropriate placement for students in advanced classes when necessary.
- Use the Iowa Acceleration Scale (Assouline et al., 2009) to assist with determining candidates eligible for acceleration.
- Provide social and emotional support to students from underserved populations who may have problems surrounding self-identity, cultural differences, poverty, or other problems that may surface as a result of their giftedness.
- Monitor the success of gifted students from underserved populations who have been placed in classes where the pace, depth, and/or complexity of the material has been modified for gifted students.
- Apprise students from underserved populations of enrichment opportunities outside the classroom, and seek ways to assist them in participating in these opportunities.
- Advocate for gifted learners from underserved populations.

# TEACHERS

- Determine the learning needs of all of the students in your classroom.
- Attend professional development sessions in gifted education to

gain a clear understanding of differentiation, enrichment, and acceleration.

- Pay particular attention to the learning strengths of students from underserved populations. Teach to their strengths while supporting areas that are not as strong.
- Embrace the belief that students can be gifted and have one or more other exceptionalities.
- Develop an understanding of the cultures represented by your students.
- Teach with a multicultural focus.
- Understand that teaching one lesson to the entire class without modifications for different levels of readiness, interest, and learning profile is not an effective practice.
- Advocate for appropriate learning environments for students from underserved populations.

# PARENTS

- Advocate for identification of and appropriate services for your gifted child.
- Make sure your child is receiving appropriate choice and challenge; your child should neither be frustrated nor bored.
- Be sure appropriate accommodations are made to address issues that may make it difficult for your child to achieve at a level commensurate with his or her ability.
- Have open communications with your child's teacher, counselor, and school administrator. Apprise them of any unusual situations or events that may be occurring in your child's home or school environment (e.g., family member incarcerated, loss of employment, victim of bullying) that may impede your child's successful performance in school.
- Seek opportunities to challenge your child outside of school.

# CONCLUSION

Suggestions for parents, teachers, administrators, and counselors who assist in meeting the needs of students include making sure that proper identification methods and instruction are provided for these students. It is critical to ensure identification measures that find those who are twice-exceptional and provide professional development for school personnel that will support students through instruction that will meet all of their needs. Support and mentoring by counselors and teachers for both students and parents is essential for this population of the gifted. Advocacy by all parties is vital in making certain that all of these recommendations are followed. Whether through identification, instruction, or support, all parties contribute to the success of learners from underserved populations.

# Suggested Resources

## DIFFERENTIATION

Adams, C. M., & Pierce, R. L. (2006). *Differentiating instruction: A practical guide to tiering lessons in the elementary grades.* Waco, TX: Prufrock Press.

Adams, C. M., & Pierce, R. L. (2010). *Differentiation that really works: Grades K–2.* Waco, TX: Prufrock Press.

Adams, C. M., & Pierce, R. L. (2010). *Differentiation that really works: Grades 3–5.* Waco, TX: Prufrock Press.

Boswell, C. A., & Carlile, V. D. (2010). *RTI for the gifted student.* Hawthorne, NJ: Educational Impressions.

Roberts, J. L., & Inman, T. (2009). *Strategies for differentiating instruction: Best practices for the classroom* (2nd ed.). Waco, TX: Prufrock Press.

Tomlinson, C. A., Brighton, C., Hertberg, H., Callahan, C., Moon, T., Brimijoin, K., . . . Reynolds, T. (2004). Differentiating instruction in response to student readiness, interest, and learning profile in academically diverse classrooms: A review of literature. *Journal for the Education of the Gifted, 27,* 119–145.

Tomlinson, C. A. (1999). *The differentiated classroom: Responding to the needs of all learners.* Alexandria, VA: ASCD.

Tomlinson, C. A. (2003). *Fulfilling the promise of the differentiated classroom: Strategies and tools for responsive teaching.* Alexandria, VA: ASCD.

# ACCELERATION:
# GENERAL RESOURCES

Assouline, S. G., Colangelo, N., Ihrig, D., Forstadt, L., Lipscomb, J., & Lupkowski-Shoplik, A. E. (2003, November). *The Iowa Acceleration Scale: Two validation studies.* Paper presented at the annual meeting of the National Association for Gifted Children, Indianapolis, IN.

Assouline, S. G., Colangelo, N., Lupkowski-Shoplik, A. E., Lipscomb, J., & Forstadt, L. (2009). *The Iowa Acceleration Scale manual* (3rd ed.). Scottsdale, AZ: Great Potential Press.

Assouline, S. G., & Lupkowski-Shoplik, A. E. (2011). *Developing math talent: A guide for educating gifted and advanced learners in math* (2nd ed.). Waco, TX: Prufrock Press.

Benbow, C. P., & Lubinski, D. (1996). *Intellectual talent: Psychometric and social issues.* Baltimore, MD: Johns Hopkins Press.

Colangelo, N., Assouline, S., & Gross, M. U. M. (2004). *A nation deceived: How schools hold back America's brightest students* (Vols. 1–2). Iowa City: The University of Iowa, The Connie Belin & Jacqueline N. Blank International Center for Gifted Education and Talent Development. (Visit http://www.accelerationinstitute.org/nation_deceived for a free download of these publications.)

Institute for Research and Policy on Acceleration, National Association for Gifted Children, & Council of State Directors of Programs for the Gifted. (2009). *Guidelines for developing an academic acceleration policy.* Iowa City, IA: Institute for Research and Policy on Acceleration. (Visit http://www.nagc.org/uploadedFiles/Advocacy/Acceleration%20Policy%20Guidelines.pdf for a free download of this publication.)

Kulik, J. A., & Kulik, C. C. (1992). Meta-analytic findings on grouping programs. *Gifted Child Quarterly, 36,* 73–77.

Muratori, M. C. (2007). *Early entrance to college: A guide to success.* Waco, TX: Prufrock Press.

National Association for Gifted Children. (2004). *Position paper: Acceleration.* Washington, DC: Author. (Visit http://www.nagc.org/uploadedFiles/PDF/Position_Statement_PDFs/pp_acceleration.pdf for a free download of this publication.)

Neihart, M. (2007). The socioaffective impact of acceleration and ability grouping. Recommendations for best practice. *Gifted Child Quarterly, 51,* 330–341.

Pressey, S. L. (1949). *Educational acceleration: Appraisals and basic problems* (Ohio State University Studies, Bureau of Educational Research Monograph No. 31). Columbus: Ohio State University Press.

Rogers, K. (2003). *Re-forming gifted education: How parents and teachers can match the program to the child.* Scottsdale, AZ: Great Potential Press.

Sayler, M. F., & Brookshire, W. K. (1993). Social, emotional, and behavioral adjustment of accelerated students, students in gifted classes, and regular students in eighth grade. *Gifted Child Quarterly, 37,* 150–154.

Schiever, S. W., & Maker, C. J. (2003). New directions in enrichment and acceleration. In N. Colangelo & G. A. Davis (Eds.), *Handbook of gifted education* (3rd ed.). Boston, MA: Allyn & Bacon.

Southern, T., & Jones, E. (Eds.). (1991). *The academic acceleration of gifted children.* New York, NY: Teachers College Press.

Swiatek, M. A., & Benbow, C. P. (1991). Ten-year longitudinal follow-up of ability-matched accelerated and unaccelerated gifted students. *Journal of Educational Psychology, 83,* 528–538.

VanTassel-Baska, J. (2005). *Acceleration strategies for teaching gifted learners.* Waco, TX: Prufrock Press.

Wells, R., Lohman, D. F., & Marron, M. A. (2009). What factors are associated with grade acceleration? An analysis and comparison of two U.S. databases. *Journal of Advanced Academics, 20,* 248–273.

# ACCELERATION: ONLINE RESOURCES

**Advanced Placement**
http://www.collegeboard.com/student/testing/ap/about.html
This site provides information about the Advanced Placement (AP) exams and courses.

**Institute for Research and Policy on Acceleration at The Connie Belin and Jacqueline N. Blank Center for Gifted Education and Talent Development**

http://www.accelerationinstitute.org

This site provides visitors information about academic acceleration for high-ability learners.

**National Association for Gifted Children**

http://www.nagc.org

This site provides position papers on acceleration, grouping, and other topics.

# ENRICHMENT: ORGANIZATIONS

**Destination ImagiNation**

http://www.destinationimagination.org

Destination ImagiNation is an organization that provides educational programs for students to learn and experience creativity, teamwork, and problem solving.

**MATHCOUNTS**

http://www.mathcounts.org

MATHCOUNTS is a national enrichment, club, and competition program that promotes middle school mathematics achievement through grassroots involvement in every U.S. state and territory.

**The Math Forum @ Drexel**

http://mathforum.org

The Math Forum @ Drexel features a wealth of problems and puzzles, online mentoring, research, team problem solving, and collaborations.

**Odyssey of the Mind**

http://www.odysseyofthemind.com

Odyssey of the Mind is an international educational program that provides creative problem-solving opportunities for students from kindergarten through college.

### The Set Daily Puzzle
http://www.setgame.com/set/puzzle_frame.htm
The Set Daily Puzzle features a new puzzle based on the Set game online every day.

# ENRICHMENT: PRECOLLEGIATE PROGRAMS

### Davidson Institute for Talent Development
http://www.davidsongifted.org
The Davidson Institute is dedicated to supporting profoundly gifted young people, their families, and the educators who serve them through free consulting services, scholarships, and summer camp.

### Duke University Talent Identification Program
http://www.tip.duke.edu
Duke TIP, a nonprofit educational organization, conducts two annual talent searches and offers summer programs, online courses, and independent learning resources.

### Gifted LearningLinks
http://www.ctd.northwestern.edu/gll
Gifted LearningLinks, run by Northwestern University's Center for Talent Development, offers academically talented students in grades K–12 the opportunity to take enrichment, high school honors, AP, and university credit courses online.

### Johns Hopkins University Center for Talented Youth
http://web.jhu.edu/cty/discover/index.html
The Center for Talented Youth offers summer and online programs for talented youth in grades K–8.

**Northwestern University's Midwest Academic Talent Search**

http://www.ctd.northwestern.edu/numats

The Midwest Academic Talent Search is a program sponsored by the Center for Talent Development at Northwestern University in Evanston, IL. NUMATS combines above-grade testing using the EXPLORE, ACT, and SAT—tests usually given to much older students—with guidance as to the appropriate academic follow-up for individual students based on their test scores.

**Summer Institute for the Gifted**

http://www.giftedstudy.org

The Summer Institute for the Gifted offers residential and day programs for gifted and talented students of ages 4–17 at college campuses across the nation.

# DICHOTOMOUS KEYS (FOR ENRICHMENT LESSONS)

**Dichotomous Key Activity**

http://www.lnhs.org/hayhurst/ips/dichot

This interactive website offers various dichotomous keys.

**Dichotomous Keys**

http://www.saskschools.ca/curr_content/biology20/unit3/unit3_mod1_les2.htm

This website contains good information about constructing dichotomous keys.

**Dichotomous Key on Norns**

http://www.biologycorner.com/worksheets/dichoto.html

This key could be used as an extension or pre- or postassessment. It uses Norns, imaginary creatures, as the organisms to be classified.

**Using a Taxonomic Key**
http://www.schools.utah.gov/curr/science/sciber00/7th/classify/sciber/taxokey.htm
This website shares how to use a dichotomous key.

# TWICE-EXCEPTIONAL

Montgomery County Public Schools. (2004). *A guidebook for twice exceptional students: Supporting the achievement of gifted students with special needs.* Retrieved from http://www.wrightslaw.com/info/2e.guidebook.pdf

**The International Dyslexia Society**
http://interdys.org
The International Dyslexia Association (IDA) is a nonprofit, scientific, and educational organization dedicated to the study and treatment of dyslexia and related language-based learning differences. This website allows you to stay up-to-date with the IDA as well as to read news and announcements, join the association, browse the online bookstore, and find an IDA member professional in any given area.

**Learning Disabilities Association of America**
http://www.ldanatl.org
Learning Disabilities Association of America's (LDA) mission is to create opportunities for success for all individuals affected by learning disabilities and to reduce the incidence of learning disabilities in future generations. The website enables you to learn about learning disabilities, look into ongoing research, see legislative updates, browse the online bookstore, join the association, and get updates on the annual conference.

**Smart Kids With Learning Disabilities**

http://www.smartkidswithld.org

Smart Kids with Learning Disabilities is a nonprofit organization dedicated to empowering the parents of children with LD and ADHD. In striving to achieve that goal, the website provides useful, authoritative information from experts, practical advice and support from parents, and inspiration from successful adults living with LD and ADHD.

**Uniquely Gifted**

http://www.uniquelygifted.org

This site is named after the book *Uniquely Gifted: Identifying and Meeting the Needs of the Twice-Exceptional Student*, edited by Kiesa Kay. This website has many links to articles of interest, information on specific special needs, other websites with general resources, and stories and personal experiences from parents and children.

# CULTURALLY, LINGUISTICALLY, AND ETHNICALLY DIVERSE STUDENTS

Boothe, D., & Stanley, J. (2004). (Eds.). *In the eyes of the beholder: Critical issues for diversity in gifted education.* Waco, TX: Prufrock Press.

Borland, J. H. (2004). *Issues and practices in the identification and education of gifted students from under-represented groups.* Storrs: University of Connecticut, The National Research Center on the Gifted and Talented.

Slocumb, P., & Payne, R. (2000). *Removing the mask: Giftedness in poverty.* Highlands, TX: Aha! Process.

The Association for the Gifted. (2009). *Diversity and developing gifts and talents: A national call to action.* Retrieved from http://www.cectag.org

VanTassel-Baska, J., & Stambaugh, T. (Eds.). (2000). *Overlooked gems: A national perspective on low income promising learners.* Washington, DC: National Association for Gifted Children.

# References

(We have identified some items listed here with D for differentiation, A for acceleration, and E for enrichment to indicate resources that further provide information on these topics.)

Adams, C. M., & Pierce, R. L. (2006). *Differentiating instruction: A practical guide to tiering lessons in the elementary grades.* Waco, TX: Prufrock Press. (D)

Anderson, L., & Krathwohl, D. (Eds.). (2001). *A taxonomy for learning, teaching, and assessing: A revision of Bloom's taxonomy of educational objectives.* New York, NY: Addison Wesley Longman. (D)

Assouline, S. G., Colangelo, N., Lupkowski-Shoplik, A., Forstadt, L., & Lipscomb, J. (2009). *Iowa Acceleration Scale manual: A guide for whole-grade acceleration K–8* (3rd ed.). Scottsdale, AZ: Great Potential Press. (A)

Berger, S. L. (1991). *Differentiating curriculum for gifted students* (ERIC Digest No. ED342175). Retrieved from http://www.ericdigests. org/1992-4/gifted.htm (D)

Bloom, B. S. (1956). *Taxonomy of educational objectives: Cognitive domain.* New York, NY: David McKay. (D)

Borland, J. H. (1997). The construct of giftedness. *Peabody Journal of Education, 72*(3&4), 6–20. (D)

Borland, J. H. (2004). *Issues and practices in the identification and education of gifted students from under-represented groups.* Storrs: University of Connecticut, The National Research Center on the Gifted and Talented. (D)

Borland, J. H., & Wright, L. (1994). Identifying young, potentially gifted, economically disadvantaged students. *Gifted Child Quarterly, 38,* 164–171. (D)

Boykin, A. W. (2000). The talent development model of schooling: Placing students at promise for academic success. *Journal of Education for Students Placed at Risk, 5,* 3–25. (D)

Caine, R., & Caine, G. (1991). *Making connections: Teaching and the human brain.* Alexandria, VA: Association for Supervision and Curriculum Development. (D)

Callahan, C. M. (2007). What can we learn from research about promising practices in developing the gifts and talents of low income students? In J. VanTassel-Baska & T. Stambaugh (Eds.), *Overlooked gems: A national perspective on low income promising learners* (pp. 53–56). Washington, DC: National Association for Gifted Children.

Colangelo, N., Assouline, S. G., & Gross, M. U. M. (2004). *A nation deceived: How schools hold back America's brightest students* (Vol. 1). Iowa City: The University of Iowa, The Connie Belin & Jacqueline N. Blank International Center for Gifted Education and Talent Development. (A)

Colangelo, N., Assouline, S. G., Marron, M. A., Castellano, J. A., Clinkenbeard, P. R., Rogers, K., . . . Smith, D. (2010). Guidelines for developing an academic acceleration policy. *Journal of Advanced Academics, 21,* 180–203. (A)

Delisle, J. (2008). Comfortably numb: A new view of underachievement. In M. W. Gosfield (Ed.), *Expert approaches to support gifted learners* (pp. 43–52). Minneapolis, MN: Free Spirit. (D)

Denbo, S. J. (2002). Institutional practices that support African American student achievement. In S. J. Denbo & L. J. Beaulieu (Eds.), *Improving schools for African American students: A reader for educational leaders* (pp. 55–71). Springfield, IL: Charles C. Thomas. (D)

Eberle, B. (2008). *Scamper.* Waco, TX: Prufrock Press. (D)

Erickson, H. L. (2002). *Concept-based curriculum and instruction.* Thousand Oaks, CA: Corwin Press. (D)

Erickson, H. L. (2007). *Concept-based curriculum and instruction for the thinking classroom.* Thousand Oaks, CA: Corwin Press. (D)

Fertig, C. (2006, November 10). What are the characteristics of effective teachers? [Blog post]. Retrieved July 13, 2011, from http://resources. prufrock.com/GiftedChildInformationBlog/tabid/57/articleType/ ArticleView/articleId/115/Default.aspx

Ford, D. Y. (2004). *Curriculum and instruction for culturally diverse gifted learners.* In C. A. Tomlinson, D. Y. Ford, S. M. Reis, C. J. Briggs, & C. A. Strickland (Eds.), *In search of the dream: Designing schools and classrooms that work for high potential students from diverse cultural backgrounds* (pp. 65–92). Washington, DC: National Association for Gifted Children.

Ford, D. Y., & Grantham, T. C. (2003). Providing access for culturally diverse gifted students: From deficit to dynamic thinking. *Theory Into Practice, 42,* 218–225. (D)

Ford, D. Y., Grantham, T. C., & Milner, H. R. (2004). Underachievement among gifted African American students: Cultural, social, and psychological considerations. In D. Boothe & J. Stanley (Eds.), *In the eyes of the beholder: Critical issues for diversity in gifted education* (pp. 15–32). Waco, TX: Prufrock Press.

Ford, D. Y., Howard, T. C., Harris, J. J., III, & Tyson, C. A. (2000). Creating culturally responsive classrooms for gifted African American students. *Journal for the Education of the Gifted, 23,* 397–427. (D)

Gallagher, J. J., Kaplan, S. N., Passow, S. H., Renzulli, J. S., Sato, I. S., Sisk, D. K., & Wickless, J. (1976). *National/State Leadership Training Institute on the Gifted and Talented.* Los Angeles, CA: Curriculum Council. (D)

Gallavan, N. P. (2000). Multicultural education at the academy: Teacher educators' challenges, conflicts, and coping skills. *Equity & Excellence in Education, 33*(3), 5–11. (D)

Gordon, W. (1971). *Synectics: The development of creative capacity.* New York, NY: Macmillan/McGraw Hill. (D)

Johnsen, S. K. (2008). Knowledge base for the 10 content standards. In S. K. Johnsen, J. VanTassel-Baska, & A. Robinson, *Using the national gifted education standards for university teacher preparation programs* (pp. 19–32). Thousand Oaks, CA: Corwin Press.

Kaplan, S. N. (1979). *In-service training manual: Activities for developing curriculum for the gifted and talented.* Los Angeles, CA: National/ State Leadership Training Institute on the Gifted and Talented. (D)

Kaplan, S. (2008). A differentiated rubric to guide teaching, learning, and assessment. In M. W. Gosfield (Ed.), *Expert approaches to support gifted learners* (pp. 101–104). Minneapolis, MN: Free Spirit. (D)

Kulik, J. A. (1992). *An analysis of the research on ability grouping: Historical and contemporary perspectives.* Storrs: University of Connecticut, The National Research Center on the Gifted and Talented. (E)

Ladson-Billings, G. (1995). Toward a theory of culturally relevant pedagogy. *American Educational Research Journal, 32,* 465–491. (D)

Latz, A. O., & Adams, C. M. (2010, May). *Critical differentiation and the twice oppressed: Social class and giftedness.* Presentation given at the 10th Biennial Wallace Research Symposium on Talent Development, Iowa City, IA. (D)

Maker, C. J. (1982). *Curriculum development for the gifted.* Rockville, MD: Aspen. (D)

Margolin, L. (1994a). A pedagogy of privilege. *Journal for the Education of the Gifted, 19,* 164–180. (D)

Margolin, L. (1994b). *Goodness personified.* New York, NY: Aldine de Gruyter. (D)

McIntosh, J., & Meacham, A. (1992). *Creative problem solving in the classroom: A teacher's guide to using CPS effectively in any classroom.* Waco, TX: Prufrock, Press. (D)

McLaren, P. (2003). Critical pedagogy: A look at the major concepts. In A. Darder, M. Baltodano, & R. Torres (Eds.), *Critical pedagogy reader* (pp. 69–96). New York, NY: Routledge. (D)

Montgomery County Public Schools. (2004). *A guidebook for twice exceptional students: Supporting the achievement of gifted students with special needs.* Retrieved from http://www.wrightslaw.com/info/2e. guidebook.pdf

Payne, R. K. (2005). *A framework for understanding poverty.* Highlands, TX: aha! Process. (D)

Rance-Roney, J. A. (2004). The affective dimension of second culture/ second language acquisition in gifted adolescents. In D. Boothe & J.

Stanley (Eds.), *In the eyes of the beholder: Critical issues for diversity in gifted education* (pp. 73–86). Waco, TX: Prufrock Press. (D)

Renzulli, J. S., & Reis, S. M. (1997). *The schoolwide enrichment model: A how-to guide for educational excellence.* Mansfield, CT: Creative Learning Press. (E)

Renzulli, J. S., & Reis, S. M. (2004). Curriculum compacting: A research-based differentiation strategy for culturally diverse talented students. In D. Boothe & J. Stanley (Eds.), *In the eyes of the beholder: Critical issues for diversity in gifted education* (pp. 87–100). Waco, TX: Prufrock Press. (A)

Renzulli, J. S., & Reis, S. M. (2006). *Enriching curriculum for all students.* Thousand Oaks, CA: Corwin Press. (E)

Roberts, J. L. (2005). *Enrichment opportunities for gifted learners.* Waco, TX: Prufrock Press. (E)

Rogers, K. (1991). *The relationship of grouping practices to the education of the gifted and talented learner.* Storrs: University of Connecticut, The National Research Center on the Gifted and Talented. (E)

Schiever, S. W., & Maker, C. J. (2003) New directions in enrichment and acceleration. In Colangelo & G. A. Davis (Eds.), *Handbook of gifted education* (3rd ed., pp. 163–173). Boston, MA: Allyn & Bacon. (E)

Slocumb, P., & Payne, R. (2000). *Removing the mask: Giftedness in poverty.* Highlands, TX: aha! Process. (D)

The Association for the Gifted, Council for Exceptional Children. (2010). *TAG's position on response to intervention for gifted children.* Retrieved from http://www.cectag.org

Texas Education Agency. (2006). *Performance standards project: Scoring dimensions.* Retrieved from http://www.texaspsp.org/exit/scoring dimensions.php?p=1

Texas Education Agency. (2010). *Texas performance standards project.* Retrieved from http://www.texaspsp.org (D)

Tomlinson, C. A. (2001). *How to differentiate instruction in mixed-ability classrooms* (2nd ed.). Alexandria, VA: ASCD. (D)

Tomlinson, C. A. (2003). *Fulfilling the promise of the differentiated classroom: Strategies and tools for responsive teaching.* Alexandria, VA: ASCD. (D)

Tomlinson, C. A. (2008). Lessons from bright learners about affect. In M. W. Gosfield (Ed.), *Expert approaches to support gifted learners* (pp. 4–9). Minneapolis, MN: Free Spirit. (D)

Tomlinson, C. A., & Strickland, C. A. (2004). Guiding the success of students of color: Themes from general education literature. In C. A. Tomlinson, D. Y. Ford, S. M. Reis, C. J. Briggs, & C. A. Strickland, *In search of the dream: Designing schools and classrooms that work for high potential students from diverse cultural backgrounds* (pp. 33–64). Washington, DC: National Association for Gifted Children.

VanTassel-Baska, J. L. (2010). Curriculum development for low-income and minority gifted learners. In J. L. VanTassel-Baska (Ed.), *Patterns and profiles of promising learners from poverty* (pp. 193–217). Waco, TX: Prufrock Press. (D)

Vialle, W., & Quigley, S. (2002). *Selective students' views of the essential characteristics of effective teachers.* Retrieved from http://www.aare.edu.au/02pap/via02437.htm

Williams, F. E. (1969). Models for encouraging creativity in the classroom by integrating the cognitive-affective domains. *Educational Technology, 9,* 7–13. (D)

# APPENDIX A

## Overcoming Obstacles: A Study of Inventors and Inventions (Grade 2)

by Trisha Oswalt

## OVERVIEW

### RATIONALE

"Overcoming Obstacles: A Study of Inventors and Inventions" is written using an Understanding by Design model (UbD; Wiggins & McTighe, 2005) with a differentiation curriculum model. This curriculum is designed for a second-grade high-ability cluster enrichment program. According to Dictionary.com, enrichment is "to add greater significance to or to supply with an abundance of anything desirable." When participating in informal discussion with my students, they are highly interested in history and inventors. Thus, this unit arose. This unit will focus on language arts reading and writing while enriching students' knowledge and love of learning through past experiences of great human beings in a UbD curriculum design.

## UNDERSTANDING BY DESIGN

The basis for the UbD philosophy is developing a deeper understanding of important ideas. It is a backward design philosophy. A designer must first focus on the desired learning, followed by thinking and planning of instruction that will challenge the students to learning success. This is often compared to travel planning. "Our frameworks should provide a set of itineraries deliberately designed to meet cultural goals rather than purposeless tour of all major sites in a foreign country" (Wiggins & McTighe, 2005, p. 14). In this philosophy, the desired results are identified in Stage 1 and known as unit goals, enduring understanding, and essential questions. In Stage 2, you will see the evidence deemed necessary to show understanding. These assessments will be informal and formal, formative and summative, and vary in multiple intelligences and learning styles. Finally, in Stage 3 of the UbD design, the learning activities, or the vehicles to which success will be derived, are listed. They are the final step in the backward design to purposefully meet the planning goals of the above stages. A WHERETO acronym will be listed to label the different strategies needed in an effective curriculum: where, what; hook and hold; equip, experience, and explore; rethink and revisit; evaluate; tailored (differentiated); and organized. UbD with differentiation is an effective philosophy in developing the curriculum for high-ability learners.

## DIFFERENTIATION

Throughout the unit, you will see various forms of differentiation. First, a quality curriculum begins with a preassessment of some sort. In this unit, preassessment will take place through both informal and formal observation. From this "testing," students will proceed with the differentiated unit lessons, or they will follow an independent learning contract that adjusts to their academic and affective needs. In the daily lessons, differentiated strategies will include flexible grouping, ongoing assessment, tiered lessons, graphic organizers, cubing, and choice boards. Accommodations will be made based on students' readiness, interest, and learning profile. During the lessons, higher level Bloom's questioning and thinking will be applied through open-ended questioning and text application to self and world. The text-to-self analysis allows me to support the emotional needs of high-ability students.

## UbD Framework Outline of "Overcoming Obstacles" Unit

**Subject Area:** Language Arts  **Grade:** Second
**Level:** High-Ability Enrichment  **Time Period:** 8+ 60-minute sessions

## Stage 1: Desired Results
### Established Goals (Standards)

- Read aloud fluently and accurately with appropriate changes in voice and expression.
- Students write clear sentences and paragraphs that develop a central idea.
- Restate facts and details or summarize the main idea in the text to clarify and organize ideas.
- Ask and respond to questions (when, who, where, why, what if, how) to aid comprehension about important elements of informational texts.
- Understand and explain common synonyms (words with the same meaning) and antonyms (words with opposite meanings).
- Use descriptive words when writing.
- Identify text that uses sequence or other logical order (alphabetical order or time).
- Identify the meaning or lesson of a story.

| Enduring Understanding(s) | Essential Question(s): |
|---|---|
| *Students will understand:* | ✓ What makes you want to listen to a reader? |
| ✓ Reading fluently and with expression makes reading more enjoyable. | ✓ What are key questions to ask when reading? |
| ✓ Summaries present the important information from an article. | ✓ What strategies will help you understand a text? |
| ✓ Asking questions helps a reader understand the text. | ✓ What life lessons can you learn from studying history? |
| ✓ Putting text in order aides understanding. | |
| ✓ History has meaning. | |
| ✓ History can encourage action. | |

| Students will know: | Students will be able to: |
|---|---|
| ✓ To use voice inflection; speak loud/ soft and fast/slow when reading aloud.<br>✓ A topic sentence is a basic sentence introducing the topic of the paragraph.<br>✓ Summarizing means restating the important points of an article. These often come from answering who, what, when, where, why, and how.<br>✓ Using synonyms creates imagery and avoids plagiarism.<br>✓ Histories of some inventors who overcame struggles in their life and changed the world. | ✓ Read a story/article fluently out loud.<br>✓ Improve their ability to create a topic sentence and descriptive details.<br>✓ Ask questions to arrive at a summary of their reading.<br>✓ Use a thesaurus to add synonyms to writing.<br>✓ Relate to the "lemons to lemonade" attitude of history and apply it on a personal level. |

## Stage 2: Assessment Evidence

### Preassessment
- Day 1 entrance and exit cards
- Final paragraphs from previous writing enrichment unit
- Day 1 class discussion, personal timeline, "Know" of a KWL chart

**Information will be used to place high-level, high-ability students in a learning contract activity and guide the designed daily lessons for the unit.

### Summative Assessment Task (GRASPS)
- Goal: Your challenge is to learn about three more inventors.
- Role: You are to work on your own and with your group.
- Audience: You need to convince your teacher that you understand the new inventor's life and inventions.
- Situation: The challenge involves dealing with others in a small-group setting and using teamwork.
- Product: You will create three products of your choice from the choice board.
- Standards: You will be assessed on your knowledge of the key points and understanding of the process of developing that information into various products.

*Ongoing Assessment (\*Differentiation)*
- Whole-group/small-group/individual discussion (\*Varied Bloom's questions)
- Observation of cubing exercise (\*Two tiers)
- Formative paragraphs
- Exit cards
- Task cards (\*Number/type of sentences)
- Timeline

*Self-Assessment*
- Think/Pair/Share reflection
- Checklist
- Exit cards

## Stage 3: Learning Activities (WHERETO Elements)

*Where Are We (Student's Point of View) Headed?*
- "Know" of KWL chart
- Inventor book skimming

*Hook*
- Voice inflection reading
- Thesaurus reading
- Sensory experience (blind)
- "Guest" speaker
- Unit role-play guessing/sharing

*Equip and Explore*
- Read aloud
- Partner reading
- Shared reading
- Cubing
- Graphic organizer
- Choice board
- Summary writing
- Descriptive writing
- Morse code inquiry
- Timeline

### Rethink and Revise
- Exit cards
- Whole-group discussion
- Peer revision

### Evaluate
- Informal observation/notes
- Think/pair/share self-evaluation
- Peer review
- Self-check exit cards

### Tailor
- Various levels of questioning
- Tiered cubes
- Grouping
- Auditory/visual/kinesthetic activities
- Various multiple intelligences activities
- Choice of summarizing processes presented

### Organize
- Day per inventor

## Resources

### Lesson 1
- *Be an Inventor* by Barbara Taylor
- *Invention* (DK Eyewitness Books) by Lionel Bender
- *So You Want to Be an Inventor?* by Judith St. George
- *A Picture Book of Amelia Earhart* by David A. Adler

### Lesson 2
- *The Real McCoy* by Wendy Towle

### Lesson 3
- *A Picture Book of Louis Braille* by David A. Adler
- *Out of Darkness: The Story of Louis Braille* by Russell Freedman

*Lesson 4*
- *Samuel Morse* by Mona Kerby

*Lesson 5*
- *Talking Leaves: The Story of Sequoyah* by Bernice Kohn
- *Sequoyah, Young Cherokee Guide* by Dorothea J. Snow

*Lesson 6*
- *Alexander Graham Bell: Inventor of the Telephone* by Time for Kids and J. Micklos, Jr.
- *Madam C. J. Walker: Pioneer Businesswoman* by Marlene Toby
- *Madam C. J. Walker* by A'Lelia Perry Bundles
- *A Picture Book of Thomas Alva Edison* by David A. Adler
- *Alexander Graham Bell and the Telephone* by Christine Webster
- *Alexander Graham Bell and the Telephone* by Steve Parker

*Lesson 8*
- *Grace Hopper: Computer Whiz* by Patricia J. Murphy
- *Click: A Story About George Eastman* by Barbara Mitchell
- *Girls Think of Everything: Stories of Ingenious Inventions by Women* by Catherine Thimmesh
- *Black Stars: African American Women Scientists and Inventors* by Otha Richard Sullivan
- *Women Invent! Two Centuries of Discoveries That Have Shaped Our World* by Susan Casey
- *Walking the Road to Freedom: A Story About Sojourner Truth* by Jeri Ferris
- *The Road to Seneca Falls* by Gwenyth Swain
- *Edith Wilson: The Woman Who Ran the United States* by James Cross Giblin

*Other*
- Video clip on Samuel Morse found at http://www.youtube.com/watch?v=oo0hSZ9R_Xk
- Morse Code online translator at http://www.onlineconversion.com/morse_code.htm

- Audiobook: *Great Inventors and Their Inventions: Gutenberg, Bell, Marconi, The Wright Brothers* by David Angus and Benjamin Soames
- DVD: *Just The Facts: Inventors That Changed America*
- Regular classroom supplies
- Material provided in the Resources section

## *Block Plan*

| Day | Objective | Evaluation | Instructional Strategy | Activities | Differentiation |
|---|---|---|---|---|---|
| 1 | Preassess and hook | Entrance/exit card, informal sharing and discussion | Whole group/ small group | Scanning, graphic organizer work | Based on info from this lesson |
| 2 | (McCoy) To understand the importance of diversity | Group discussion/informal cubing observation | Read aloud | Discussion chart/cubing | Tiered cubes |
| 3 | (Braille) To model summarizing | Discussion, graphic organizer, task card | Read aloud, modeling | Graphic organizer/ task card | Open-ended task, text-to-self connections |
| 4 | (Morse) Add synonyms to summaries | Formative paragraphs | Inquiry partner work | Partner reading, summarizing, video clip | Learning styles: kinesthetic, visual, auditory |
| 5 | (Sequoyah) To understand the effectiveness of timelines | Exit card, timeline | Shared reading, storytelling | Timeline, discussion | Discussion, level of questioning |
| 6–8 | (Bell, Walker, Edison) A summative look at understanding of all skills and standards | Choice board products | Small-group rotations | Reading, choice boards | Choice boards |
| 9–? | Extension/ advancement of unit | Summary of inventor, application to self | Independent study | Learning contract | Nature of assignment |

## *Preassessment: Day 1*

### *Topical Enduring Understanding*

- We must see what we know before we can know where we are heading.

### *Topical Essential Question*

- What do we know about timelines, reading aloud, synonyms, and history?

### *Focus Objective*

- The teacher will understand what the students know and set the stage for learning about history.

### *Lesson*

1. Use the final paragraph from a recently finished writing sample to check for writing ability and understanding.
2. Entrance card: Have students complete a timeline of four events that have happened in second grade. Allow students time to share, then collect (check sequence). (See Resources section.)
3. Place invention books on tables. Give students 5 minutes to scan the books. Allow all students to share one interesting fact (check for fluency and inflection). Question students for different words that could be used in the facts they read (check for synonyms).
4. Think-Pair-Share: Read inventors aloud to students from board. Have students partner together to come up with anything they know about the inventors. Share with the class (list on the board).
5. Depending on availability, show a portion of the *Inventors That Changed America* DVD to hook students into the unit and excite them about America's history. If the DVD is not available, read aloud about Amelia Earhart and discuss the hardships she faced and overcame.
6. Exit card: Have students write down one thing they want to know about one of the listed inventors.

Use this information to determine any students who may need the independent study learning contract verses regular enrichment work. Also, use the information to guide the lessons.

## Lesson 1: Day 2 (Elijah McCoy)

### Focus Standards

- Read aloud fluently and accurately with appropriate changes in voice and expression.
- Restate facts and details or summarize the main idea in the text to clarify and organize ideas.
- Ask and respond to questions (when, who, where, why, what if, how) to aid comprehension about important elements of informational texts.
- Identify the meaning or lesson of a story.

### Topical Enduring Understanding

- McCoy faced the challenge of diversity with courage.

### Topical Essential Question

- What obstacles did McCoy have to overcome as an inventor?

### Objectives

- The learner will know the importance of reading fluently and with expression.
- The learner will be able to comprehend higher level text by asking questions.
- The learner will value the meaning of equality.

### Anticipatory Set

- Have a statement on the table for students to read. (Billy asked, "Have you heard of the real McCoy?" Susie responded, "No, can you tell me about it?") Have students go around the table and read the statement aloud. Ask students which person they enjoyed listening to and what they enjoyed about it. Direct students to the importance of fluency, voice inflection, and confidence (write on board). Explain that you will be reading aloud today and they will get a chance to hear the three described items.

*Lesson*

1. Read aloud *The Real McCoy* by Wendy Towle. Pause during story to answer questions, develop schema, and aid understanding.
2. Put on "understanding glove" (see Resources section). As a group, answer the questions on the glove with chart paper (complete sentences). Post the answers on the wall. Place special emphasis on the "heart/lesson" of the story.
   - Who: Elijah McCoy was an African American engineer and inventor. He was the son of runaway slaves who made it to Canada.
   - When: He lived during the Civil War and post Civil War time period.
   - Where: He went to school in Europe. He settled in Michigan.
   - Why: McCoy was interested in mechanical devices and how things worked. His parents valued education.
   - What: He developed several inventions, such as the oil cup.
   - How: McCoy had to sell his patents to earn money to continue inventing.
   - Heart: Despite an unequal society, McCoy never gave up on his passion and dreams.

3. Return students to two tables and present a cubing activity. Table 1 will receive a lower level Bloom's cube, while Table 2 will receive a higher level Bloom's cube (see Resources section). Use informal observation to place students at the tables.
4. Wrap up the lesson by having students reread their intro statement with reading aloud skills and provide an answer to the question read.

## Lesson 2: Day 3 (Louis Braille)

*Focus Standard*

- Restate facts and details or summarize the main idea in the text to clarify and organize ideas.

*Topical Essential Question*

- What is a summary?

### Topical Enduring Understandings
- Summaries present the important information from an article.
- Asking questions helps a reader understand the text.

### Objective
- The learner will know that summarizing means restating the important points of an article. These often come from answering who, what, when, where, why, and how.

### Anticipatory Set
- As students walk in to take their seats, blindfold two or three students. Have another student help them to their seats. Explain that today's inventor is a person who was unable to use his sense of sight. Have students stay blindfolded during the story.

### Lesson
1. Read aloud *A Picture Book of Louis Braille* by David A. Adler. Give students a chance to demonstrate reading aloud during different pages.
2. Discuss obstacles and the importance of Braille. Allow students to feel the Braille at the end of the book.
3. Give each student a "hamburger" graphic organizer (see Resources section). Show students this technique for summarizing the key points in the story. If this model is new to students, complete the activity as a whole group, modeling this new organizer with the 5W (who, what, when, where, why) and 1H (how) words to find key ideas.
4. Present a Beautiful Picture Task (I chose a Thomas Kincaid painting to display):

   *You have just signed up for a Braille contest to help a fellow class-mate. Your task is to describe the picture in five sentences to a person who can't see it. Use lots of adjectives and synonyms to help create the picture in the mind of the person. If your sentences are chosen as the winning description, we will turn them into Braille to help those who can't see! Good luck!*

5. Give students time to complete and share if time permits.

## Lesson 3: Day 4 (Samuel Morse)

### Focus Standard

- Understand and explain common synonyms (words with the same meaning) and antonyms (words with opposite meanings).

### Topical Enduring Understanding

- Synonyms can improve a summary by adding descriptive detail.

### Topical Essential Question

- What is a thesaurus used for and how can it help us?

### Objectives

- The learner will understand how to use a thesaurus to help his or her writing. (Associated standard: Using synonyms creates imagery and avoids plagiarism.)
- The learner will practice reading and summarizing a compiled article about Samuel Morse. (Associated standards: A topic sentence is a basic sentence introducing the topic of the paragraph; Summarizing means restating the important points of an article. These often come from answering who, what, when, where, why, and how.)

### Anticipatory Set

- Have several thesauri on the tables. Explain and examine the use of a thesaurus. Have students race to look up synonyms to the following words:
  - o good
  - o bad
  - o happy
  - o mad

  The first person to find the given word and its synonym should stand up and put the book on his or her head (no talking). Wrap up this hook by discussing the importance of synonyms.

*Lesson*

1. Show students a video clip on Samuel Morse.
2. Give students an inquiry riddle written in Morse code and a key to decode it. Allow students to work in partners to decipher, "What obstacles were in Samuel Morse's life?"
3. Once students have cracked the code correctly, give students time to read an article about Alfred Vail and Samuel Morse. Walk around and provide feedback on voice inflection and reading aloud. Check for understanding.
4. Give students a checklist and hamburger graphic organizer that they and their peers will use to edit their paper. Have students summarize the obstacles Morse overcame in a paragraph with synonyms from "describing words" (adjectives) found in the article. Have students finish the lesson by decoding one sentence from their paragraph in Morse code. Have students ask one other group to review their summary before turning it in (use checklist).
5. In a whole group, wrap up the lesson by verbalizing the key points with the "understanding glove."
6. Extension: Visit an online translator and translate the summary paragraph (see Resources section). Provide extra books on the subject for those interested.

## Lesson 4: Day 5 (Sequoyah)

*Focus Standards*

- Identify text that uses sequential or other logical order (alphabetical or chronological order).
- Identify the meaning or lesson of a story.

*Topical Enduring Understanding*

- Putting text in order aids understanding.

*Topical Essential Question*

- How will ordering the story of Sequoyah help me understand her life?

*Objectives*
- The learner will understand the events that led up to Sequoyah's invention and the need for her invention.
- The learner will understand that timelines are an essential reference to understanding the events in a person's life.

*Anticipatory Set*
- When students enter the classroom, have directions on the board for them to find their name card and a copy of *Talking Leaves: The Story of Sequoyah* by Bernice Kohn and begin looking through it. The teacher will enter within minutes of their arrival dressed as Sequoyah. Encourage them to sit on the floor for an oral story telling of the book (have them follow along with their copies).

*Lesson*
1. Begin telling the story of Sequoyah as memorized from the text. Encourage students to read certain parts of the text and talk about it. Discuss the importance of oral tradition to Native Americans and "your" (Sequoyah's) impact on writing down information as well.
2. Discuss with students the importance of drawing as seen in the text. Bring out an empty timeline and ask students to help fill in the events of "your" life, adding words and pictures of five important details; discuss the 5W and 1H questions as part of determining importance. Teach students the use of lines to mark time. Label each detail with the time and a summary. Complete the timeline together on butcher paper size.
3. Exit card: Ask students to identify the big idea (overcoming obstacles/being successful) of all of the stories they have read thus far. Next, ask which one was the most inspiring to them and why.

## Lesson 5: Days 6–8 (Performance Task: Choice Board)

*Standard*
- Culmination of all standards combined

*Topical Enduring Understanding*
- Culmination of all enduring understandings

*Topical Essential Question*
- Culmination of all essential questions

*Objective*
- The learner will do independent practice of all skills learned to show developing mastery.

*Anticipatory Set*
- (Basically a share time from last lesson's exit card.) Have the names Elijah McCoy, Samuel Morse, Louis Braille, and Sequoyah on the tables. Ask students to pick one name and be prepared to tell one thing they learned or liked about their chosen person. They can also role-play something the inventor would have done.

*Lesson*
1. Tell students that today is going to be the start of a three-session project. Present the three remaining inventors: Madam C. J. Walker, Alexander Graham Bell, and Thomas Alva Edison and the choice board. Explain that students will be rotating through each of the inventor's stations, and that while there, they must choose one activity on their choice board to do at each station. Present the choice board and the activities (see Resources section). Show the "toolbox" spot in the room where all necessary materials may be gathered.
2. Discuss the need for indoor voices while at each station. Discuss the "Ask 3 (in group) before me" rule, telling students you will be around to guide each group as you can.
3. Divide students into tiered groups based on data collected in previous lessons on development of skills and standards. Begin learning.
4. Each of the three sessions will be spent with one inventor. Students may read the presented information as a group, with a partner, or on their own as desired. When a video clip is available, they must

watch it together. Each student will be responsible for turning in three final products, but the students may work together to help each other as needed.

5. Wrap up each day by allowing for whole-group discussion on their learning for the day (have them describe their learning experience in terms such as interesting, surprising, disappointing, and so forth).

## Lesson 6: Independent Activity for Differentiation or Extension Project for High-Ability Students: Learning Contract

### Standard

- Restate facts and details or summarize the main idea in the text to clarify and organize ideas.
- Ask and respond to questions (when, who, where, why, what if, how) to aid comprehension about important elements of informational texts.
- Identify the meaning or lesson of a story.
- Write clear sentences and paragraphs that develop a central idea.
- Understand and explain common synonyms (words with the same meaning) and antonyms (words with opposite meanings).
- Use descriptive words when writing.

### Topical Enduring Understanding

- Learning from an historical perspective about overcoming obstacles can give meaning to my life.

### Topical Essential Question

- What happened in the life of _____ and how can I relate it to myself?

### Objective

- The learner will enhance his or her knowledge of overcoming obstacles from an historical perspective in an independent learning style.

- The learner will understand the life, obstacles, and invention of a new (to them) inventor.
- The learner will apply the concept of life, obstacles, hard work, and success to his or her life.
- The learner will write an autobiography forecasting the rest of his or her life as an inventor.
- The learner will understand the hard work of creating inventions.

### Background

- Students who will be participating in this learning contract are students who showed great understanding of inventors involved in the preassessment. If no students fit into this category during preassessment but show tremendous growth and interest during the unit, this may be an extension to the unit for all high-ability students.

### Activities

- The student(s) will choose an unfamiliar inventor from a provided list.
- The student(s) will research the inventor from a provided book (optional Internet time may be available). Students are always encouraged to attain books on their own but are not required to do so.
- The student(s) will summarize the life of the inventor, including the obstacles he or she had to overcome, the attitude that led to success, and the invention and its lasting effects on our life today.
- The student(s) will apply the knowledge about an inventor's life to themselves. They will brainstorm about the different parts of their life and then translate it into a book. An empty book will be provided for the students with the different parts of their life sequenced for them (childhood, adulthood, struggles, invention success, leaving a legacy).
- If there is access to the computers, students may complete the book with Kid Pix or similar software.
- The student(s) will create the invention they aspired to in their autobiography. This may be a drawing or an actual object.

*Resources*
- Inventor books and summary rubric
- Miscellaneous paper, objects, pipe cleaners, and the like for invention and rubric
- Paper and pencils
- Book template and rubric

*Product/Outcome*
- The product will be a one-paragraph summary of the chosen inventor.
- The product will be an autobiography book three to four pages in length (with a fair understanding of paragraphs).
- The product will be a created invention that reflects the life lived in the autobiography.

*Evaluation Criteria*
- Checklists will be used for the summary, autobiography, and invention.
- Informal evaluation will take place during the unit.

# Reference

Wiggins, G., & McTighe, J. (2005). *Understanding by design* (2nd ed.). Alexandria, VA: ASCD.

# RESOURCES

## *Day 1*

## *Entrance Card*

**Directions:** Fill in the timeline below with four events that have happened to you this year in second grade.

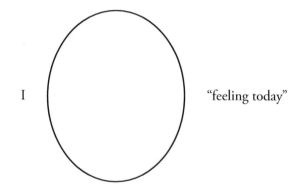

## *Exit Card*

I     (     )     "feeling today"

Write one sentence telling me something you *want to know* about one of the inventors.

# *Day 2*

Billy asked, "Have you heard of the real McCoy?"
Susie responded, "No, can you tell me about it?"

## *Simulation of the Understanding Glove*

This is an inexpensive cotton glove, easily found at any retail store. Each finger has the word *who, what, when/where, why,* and *how* written on it, with the *heart of the story* in the palm written in marker or puffy paint.

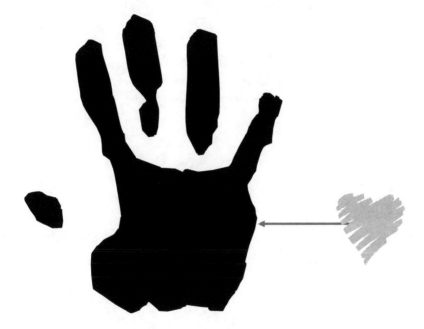

## Tiered Cubes 1

How would you feel
if you were McCoy?

What would be
McCoy's favorite
part of living in
America today?

What was the main
thing that kept McCoy
from being successful?

How did McCoy's
wife work to overcome
inequality?

Describe one of
McCoy's inventions.

What would you
say to McCoy if you
could meet him?

## *Tiered Cube 2*

Use three adjectives to describe McCoy's personality.

Should McCoy have accepted such a low price for his patents? Why or why not?

Share one difference in America as it is today versus America as described in the story.

How did his wife work to overcome inequality?

Select one part of the story and tell how it demonstrated inequality.

Select one invention and explain how it has helped you or your family.

## Day 3

### Graphic Organizer: Hamburger Model

Topic Sentence

Detail

Detail

Detail

Conclusion

## *Beautiful Picture Task*

**Directions:** You have just signed up for a Braille contest to help a fellow classmate. Your task is to describe the picture in five sentences to a person who can't see it. Use lots of adjectives and synonyms to help create the picture in the mind of the person. If your sentences are chosen as the winning description, we will turn them into Braille to help those who can't see. Good luck!

# *Day 4*

## *Morse Code Riddle*

**Directions:** Your mission is to decode the following Morse code message and then answer the question it asks you based on your reading today.

.--    ....    .-    -

\_\_\_    \_\_\_    \_\_\_    \_\_\_

---    -...    ...    -    .-    -.-.    .-..    .    ...

\_\_\_    \_\_\_    \_\_\_    \_\_\_    \_\_\_    \_\_\_    \_\_\_    \_\_\_    \_\_\_

.--    .    .-.    .

\_\_\_    \_\_\_    \_\_\_    \_\_\_

..    -.

\_\_\_    \_\_\_

...    .-    --    ..-    .    .-..

\_\_\_    \_\_\_    \_\_\_    \_\_\_    \_\_\_    \_\_\_

--    ---    .-.    ...    .    ...

\_\_\_    \_\_\_    \_\_\_    \_\_\_    \_\_\_ ,    \_\_\_

.-..    ..    ..-.    .

\_\_\_    \_\_\_    \_\_\_    \_\_ ?

The International Morse code characters are:

| A | .- | N | -. | 0 | ----- |
|---|-----|---|-----|---|-------|
| B | -... | O | --- | 1 | .---- |
| C | -.-. | P | .--. | 2 | ..--- |
| D | -.. | Q | --.- | 3 | ...-- |
| E | . | R | .-. | 4 | ....- |
| F | ..-. | S | ... | 5 | ..... |
| G | --. | T | - | 6 | -.... |
| H | .... | U | ..- | 7 | --... |
| I | .. | V | ...- | 8 | ---.. |
| J | .--- | W | .-- | 9 | ----. |
| K | -.- | X | -..- | | |
| L | .-.. | Y | -.-- | | |
| M | -- | Z | --.. | | |

Visit the following websites to learn about Samuel Morse and Alfred Vail:

- http://www.bookrags.com/biography/alfred-vail-woi
- http://web.mit.edu/invent/iow/morse.html

Once you have done so, summarize what you have read below.

## *Alfred Vail/Samuel Morse Summary*

_____

_____

_____

_____

_____

## Summary Checklist

Author: _____

Peer Edit Partner: _____

| Qualities of a Summary | Author Check | Peer Check | Teacher Check |
|---|---|---|---|
| Does the summary have a topic sentence? | | | |
| Does the summary answer who, what, when, where, why, and how? | | | |
| Does the summary have a closing sentence? | | | |
| Does the summary have all of its capitals and periods? | | | |
| What did you enjoy while reading this summary? | | | |
| What words are synonyms for a word in your reading?<br>*<br><br>*<br><br>* | | | |

# *Day 5*

## *Exit Card*

What is the big idea of our inventor study?

_____

_____

_____

_____

Which inventor was the most inspiring to you? Why?

_____

_____

_____

_____

_____

_____

# *Day 6*

## *Inventor Choice Board*

**Directions:** Choose one activity in the board at each inventor station. Your chosen activities must make a tic-tac-toe. When you are finished, turn this paper in with your completed tasks. If you have extra time, you may do more than three activities. Have fun!

| | | |
|---|---|---|
| Create a three-section comic strip summarizing what you read about _____. | Write a summary paragraph about what you read about _____. | Draw a picture about a time in your life when you felt like _____. |
| Make a puppet about _____ and have him tell the class three important details about what you read. | Create a collage of words and their synonyms that would describe the life of _____. | Design a poster about the invention of _____. |
| Hypothesize (guess) what might have changed if the person were living today. Write at least three sentences. | Write a paragraph that might have been out of the journal/diary of _____. | Create a time-line for the life of _____. |

## *Station #1*

### Madam C. J. Walker

1. Log onto the computer and visit http://www.madamcjwalker. com.
2. Make sure to read the student section and the frequently asked questions.
3. Read through the books provided on her life for additional information.
4. Complete one choice board task.

## *Station #2*

### Alexander Graham Bell

1. View an animated version of the beginning of Bell's telephone invention at http://www.youtube.com/watch?v=2BCvXH5M9n0.
2. Read through the books provided to understand Bell's life, the obstacles he had to overcome, and his invention.
3. Complete one choice board activity.

## *Station #3*

### Thomas Alva Edison

1. Begin by reading the picture book on Edison's life.
2. Browse through the other books as time allows.
3. You may also go to a Yahoo! Kids search engine and type in Thomas Alva Edison to learn more.
4. Complete one choice board activity.

## *Learning Contract*

Welcome to an exciting independent project about inventors! When working on your project, please remember:

- Work hard!
- Ask questions during teacher conferences.
- If other students are also doing a project, be sure to "ask three before me."
- Use an inside voice if talking.
- Use the table below to complete all parts of your project.
- Use the handouts provided to help you complete your projects.

I understand the expectations placed before me.

_____ (student)

I understand the expectations placed before my student.

_____ (parent)

I am confident _____ can do this!

_____ (teacher)

| Assignments | Teacher Check | Parent Check |
|---|---|---|
| 1. Choose an inventor unfamiliar to you from the list provided. | | |
| 2. Read at least two different articles about your chosen inventor. Use the books provided, research from your own books, or Internet articles. | | |
| 3. Write a one-page paper summarizing the life of the inventor, including the obstacles that person had to overcome, the attitude that led to his or her success, and the invention and its lasting effects on our lives. | | |
| 4. Brainstorm an invention you would create as an inventor. | | |
| 5. Imagine your life as the inventor of _____. Write your autobiography. Brainstorm the different parts of your life and how they might be similar to the inventor you studied. Think about your (made-up) childhood, adulthood, struggles, invention success, and leaving a legacy. | | |
| 6. Create a picture book about your life using your brainstorm. | | |
| 7. Create your invention to be displayed with your book. | | |

## *Inventor List*

**Directions:** Choose one inventor from the following list. You may browse through the books to help you decide.

- Helen Blanchard: zig-zag stitching on sewing machines
- Dr. Grace Murray Hopper: COBOL computer language
- Marion Donovan: disposable diaper
- Ruth Wakefield: chocolate chip cookies
- Art Fry: Post-It® Notes
- George Eastman: Kodak
- Johannes Gutenberg: printing press
- Guglielmo Marconi: radio
- Other (see me): _____

**Checklist for Written Summary of** _____

| Include | Self-Check | Teacher Check |
|---|---|---|
| 1. Summary includes a topic sentence, closing sentence, and details. | | |
| 2. Details answer who, what, when, where, why, and how. | | |
| 3. Details include the obstacles that person had to overcome, the attitude that led to his or her success, and the invention and its lasting effects on our lives. | | |
| 4. (Extra) I looked up synonyms to add to my summary. | | |
| 5. My favorite part: | | |
| 6. The hardest part: | | |

## Inventor Autobiography Book Checklist

| Include | Self-Check | Teacher Check |
|---|---|---|
| 1. Book has a title, picture, and author on the front. | | |
| 2. Book has a page with three or more sentences on each subtopic: childhood, adulthood, struggles, and invention success. | | |
| 3. Book has illustrations to highlight the autobiography. | | |
| 4. The book shows hard work and good effort. | | |
| 5. My favorite part: | | |
| 6. The hardest part: | | |

**Invention Checklist**

| Include | Self-Check | Teacher Check |
|---|---|---|
| 1. Invention compares to the initial brain-storm and matches the autobiography. | | |
| 2. Invention shows creativity. | | |
| 3. Invention shows hard work and good effort. | | |
| 4. My favorite part: | | |
| 5. The hardest part: | | |

## *Option 1 for Inventor Brainstorm*

**Inventor's Name:** _____

| Childhood | Adulthood |
|---|---|
|  |  |
|  |  |
| **Struggles** | **Inventions and Successes** |
|  |  |

*Option 2 for Inventor Brainstorm*

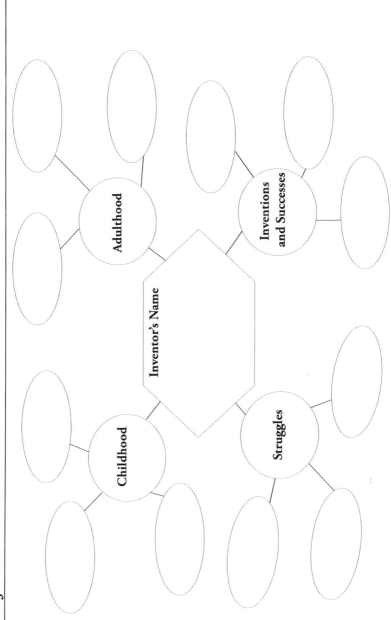

# About the Authors

**Cheryll M. Adams** is the Director of the Center for Gifted Studies and Talent Development at Ball State University. She teaches graduate courses for the license in gifted education. For the past 30 years, she has served in the field of gifted education as a teacher of gifted students at all grade levels; Director of Academic Life at the Indiana Academy for Science, Mathematics, and Humanities; and as the principal teacher in the Ball State Institute for the Gifted in Mathematics program. Additionally, she has been the founder and director of various other programs for gifted students. Dr. Adams has authored or coauthored numerous publications in professional journals, as well as several book chapters. She serves on the editorial review board for *Roeper Review, Gifted Child Quarterly, Journal for the Education of the Gifted,* and *The Teacher Educator.* She has served on the Board of Directors of the National Association for Gifted Children, has been president of the Indiana Association for the Gifted, and currently serves on the board of The Association for the Gifted, Council for Exceptional Children. In 2002, she received the NAGC Early Leader Award.

**Cecelia Boswell** is the founder of Austin Creek Education Systems (ACES). She has more than 35 years of experience in public school classroom teaching and as consultant and liaison to local education agencies with the Texas Education Agency, Advanced Academic Services Division. Since founding ACES, she has worked as a consultant with the Florida

Department of Education, multiple independent school districts and Education Service Centers across Texas, and the Texas Education Agency. She has audited and facilitated restructure of advanced academics services in a variety of Texas school districts. She has been invited to speak at the World Conference on the Gifted, the International Association for Curriculum Development conference, and the International Conference for North America and the Caribbean, International Baccalaureate. She has served on the board and as the president of the Texas Association for the Gifted and Talented, the awards committee of the National Association for Gifted Children, and the board of The Association for the Gifted, Council for Exceptional Children. In 2001, she received the Edward B. Chance Dissertation of the Year Award from the National Rural Education Association.